THE FAST FOUNDER

THE EAST INDIAMAN

THE

FROM STARTUP

FAST

TO EXIT IN

36 MONTHS

FOUNDER

ERIC LAM

Marshall Cavendish
Business

Published by Marshall Cavendish Business
An imprint of Marshall Cavendish International

A member of the
Times Publishing Group

Other Marshall Cavendish Offices
Marshall Cavendish Corporation, 800 Westchester Ave, Suite N-641,
Rye Brook, NY 10573, USA • Marshall Cavendish International (Thailand)
Co Ltd, 253 Asoke, 16th Floor, Sukhumvit 21 Road, Klongtoey Nua,
Wattana, Bangkok 10110, Thailand • Marshall Cavendish (Malaysia)
Sdn Bhd, Times Subang, Lot 46, Subang Hi-Tech Industrial Park,
Batu Tiga, 40000 Shah Alam, Selangor Darul Ehsan, Malaysia

Marshall Cavendish is a registered trademark of Times Publishing Limited

National Library Board, Singapore Cataloguing in Publication Data

Name(s): Lam, Eric, 1972-
Title: The fast founder : from start-up to exit in 36 months / Eric Lam.
Description: Singapore : Marshall Cavendish Business, [2023]
Identifier(s): ISBN 978-981-5113-12-9
Subject(s): LCSH: Entrepreneurship. | New business enterprises--Management.
Classification: DDC 658.421--dc23

Printed in Singapore

To my lovely wife, Christine,
who never once stopped believing in me
and my ability to change the world,
even as my world collapsed around me in tough times.
She is by far my most precious investor!

CONTENTS

Prologue

I was once part of a panel of three founders, who were invited by a reputable university in the region to share our experiences as founders and entrepreneurs with visiting MBA students. With me was an ex-investment banker turned entrepreneur and a high-flying entrepreneur who was on the Forbes 30 under 30 list. One of the students asked us whether we had ever thought of giving up on our journey.

"I cannot afford to let these thoughts enter my brain. I just have to keep moving forward," replied the ex-investment banker turned entrepreneur.

"If I had thought about it, I wouldn't have been able to build my company to what it is now. I would have been too tempted to give up," said the Forbes 30 under 30 founder.

When it was my turn, I told them that I had such thoughts every other day, especially when I felt my venture wasn't going anywhere. But what I feel and what I decide to do are two very different things. I explained:

> When I decided to start my venture and become an entrepreneur, I decided that I wouldn't give up until I was quite certain that it would be the best thing to do for everyone and for myself. As the sun sets on a fruitless and even a bad day, I may grieve over the losses I have incurred that day.
>
> As I go to bed that night and wake up when the sun rises, I know that it's a new day, with new beginnings, new opportunities, new challenges and new trophies for

the taking. I don't give up and I go out to hunt again. Because this is what I have decided for myself when I started my venture.

The students applauded. I'm not sure why. Maybe it's because of what I said or how I said it that somehow moved them.

But make no mistake – there is nothing romantic or heroic about starting a new venture, on being a founder, an entrepreneur. These days, the mass media glorifies the triumphs of successful founders and some even think that entrepreneurship is a rite of passage in a holistic tertiary education.

I disagree with this paradigm, because not everyone is called to be an entrepreneur or a founder of new ventures.

Entrepreneurs are a strange breed. We are social misfits. We seem unable to work with others in a team. Yet, we have a crazy allegiance to team members who are under our care in our enterprise. We feel disproportionately responsible for them because they have agreed to come on board with us, sacrificing an otherwise better paying job to help us build our dream. We have an insatiable desire to change the world and we are prepared to put everything on the line to make it happen.

Even as we fail, we don't stop.

So, for those who feel a calling to embark on this incredible journey filled with swings towards both triumph and tragedy, sometimes all within the same day, maybe even at the same moment, I'd like to think that you may appreciate a concise account of the lessons one person has learned from starting and exiting a few ventures of his own and from the conversations he has had with other entrepreneurs, investors and advisors.

If so, then this book is for you.

In this book, I hope you will be able to find a compass and a road map to start your own venture, grow it and exit it – all in 36 months. And because you're an entrepreneur, you won't stop there but will move on to find the next big problem to solve, to better society and the world we live in.

I have tried to address the concerns of new venture founders, especially first-time founders, in the three aspects of starting a new venture: the Paradigm, the Plan, and the Execution. Over these sections of the book, I challenge the founder to have a paradigm of launching fast, failing fast, learning fast and exiting fast. On the plan, I share my personal experiences and those of others to help the founder with ideas to win in a crowded business environment and to provide a customer experience so delightful that it is audaciously desirable. In executing the venture idea, I hope to provide the founder with recommendations on how to bring the best resources on board and how to go to market and score the first customers without having to spend like crazy, and what financial metrics to look at to grow and exit the business.

Since this won't be your last venture, you might as well get it up running fast, and exit it before it takes a toll on your life and makes you think that you're too old to solve the next problem.

I have used the words "enterprise" and "company" interchangeably to mean organisations that exert a social (may or may not make money) or commercial (make money) impact on society. I have used the word "venture" to refer to any business that can exist on its own as a company or as a special business unit within an organisation. Thus, a new venture can exist within an existing enterprise and some enterprises do pivot from one venture to another, depending on the successes of those ventures. I consider anyone who starts a venture to be a founder. I have masked the names of individuals and private companies, whose experiences with growing new ventures and dealing with investors have provided me with many insights, enabling me to share them in this book.

The mandate to startup and exit in 36 months demands that founders work hard and smart to get their products to the market and into the hands of their customers at rocket speed. They have to learn fast to figure out what works with their customers and what needs tweaking. They must act decisively to grow their businesses without burning themselves to the ground. And they do so with the intent to create, grow and exit a new venture in 36 months.

These are the Fast Founders. And this book is about their mindsets, strategies and practices.

Not everyone will agree with everything I have written in this book, but I certainly hope you will enjoy reading it as much as I have enjoyed writing it.

SECTION 1
THE PARADIGM

1

The 36-3 Mandate

The Tale of Two Edtechs

AnalyzeEdu and LanguageStories are two education technology companies with a mission to change the way teachers work and learners learn. Both are led by highly energetic founders.

AnalyzeEdu seeks to relieve teachers in schools from menial tasks so that they can focus on teaching. The founders reason that teachers join the teaching profession to teach and not to do these "extracurricular activities" that distract them from their core work. The company's online platform also has a feature to detect children whose mental health may be at risk, through daily check-in reflections on the platform. This, they reckon, is an important piece of information for teachers, enabling them to be on the lookout for children who might be struggling with mental health issues or are suffering from abnormal amounts of stress. They shared that the company has been around for slightly over four years, and they have a ten per cent share of the public school market. Its annual revenue is less than $200,000. The company is slightly profitable. According to the founders, most of their clients have come to them by word of mouth from existing clients.

LanguageStories is on a mission to help young children learn a language in a highly engaging way and the company has produced learning material for its teachers to conduct online lessons. The company has been around for two years and is grossing revenue of less than $180,000 annually. The founders have recently called their customers and derived a net promoter score of 8.7 (I will share more about the relevance of this data in later chapters). Additionally, it costs the company $250 to acquire one customer, who pays $130 for one month's worth of online lessons. The company is making a loss, burning cash each month and is about to run out of money. The founders therefore decided to retrench 70 per cent of their team, leaving just three people to run the operations. They figured that this could let them survive for a longer period until they receive fresh funds.

Both companies want to grow and the founders feel that raising funds is the best option. Both have the potential to succeed. But, in my opinion, one of them should either close or drastically pivot, while the other should consider doubling down big time.

So which company should do what?

The 36-3 Mandate

Before we agree to work with entrepreneurs to build a new business venture, we often need to get their agreement to the "36-3 mandate". **At the end of 36 months of starting the venture, we must be able to answer "yes" to at least one of the following three questions:**

1. Are we in a position to sell the venture?
2. Can we float the venture in the stock exchange (launch an IPO)?
3. Should we close and wind up the venture?

There should be nothing in between as anything else will mean dragging our feet for another potentially long period of our lives, only to see the venture possibly ending up in the same place much further down the road (and our mortal lives are too short for that). If we are unsure of the answers to any of these questions by the 36th month, we can, at most, give ourselves another 12 months (a "+12" allowance), but by the 48th month, we must make one of these three decisions.

The Best and Worst Types of Businesses to Run

It was spring of 2018 and I was meeting one of the investors in my previous venture along the scenic banks of the West Lake (西湖) in Hangzhou, China. Having succeeded in running a business whose value had once reached more than $1 billion, I had a lot to learn from him and he was generous and patient in sharing with me his experience and battle scars. We talked about the plans for my enterprise and towards the end of our meeting, he eluded to me that "the worst type of business to run is one that makes too little to succeed, and loses too little to fail."

He elaborated that it is always good news to an entrepreneur when one of the following two outcomes takes place in any business:

- Outcome 1: the company makes so much money that its owners can sell it or continue to grow it; or
- Outcome 2: the company has lost and is continuing to lose so much money that it makes more sense to close it before it's too late.

According to him, these two outcomes would clearly help an entrepreneur to decide on what to do next.

Then there is Outcome 3:

> It is the third outcome of not failing enough and not making enough that traps many entrepreneurs. It places the enterprise in a zombie state, too healthy to die, yet too sick to live.

There is wisdom in these words, but it takes a huge toll on a founder to act on it, simply because it takes all of our dreams and waking moments to nurture our enterprise, this baby of ours, and having to end it is a tough call.

Of course, many entrepreneurs before us have grown successful businesses on pivots from their original offerings while some have persevered to success. I can think of Rovio (the creators of the Angry Birds franchise) and Pinterest, to name two examples.

As entrepreneurs, we celebrate our ability to persevere, to demonstrate grit, determination and passion to get the job done when the going gets tough. Nothing of what I have written so far diminishes any of these qualities. We must have them if we want to change the world. But having the right mindset from the start is vital if we want to grow any new venture in a productive and pragmatic way. And preparing ourselves to face the above three questions at the end of a limited period will help us to frame our thinking with an end in mind, whatever that end may be, and a timeline of 36 months is just about right for a company to reach that state. At worst, if we need to face the inevitable closure, at least we are prepared for it. True entrepreneurs do not stop seeking to solve problems in the world they live in, and one business closure shouldn't stop us from starting another soon after.

I'm not, however, saying that we have to sell our enterprise or float it on the stock market if it is so successful by the end of the 36 months, but having this goal means we are poised to better plan for it, and having the option to do so then means that we would be in a better position to grow it further by that time.

Six "Must-Haves" in any Successful New Venture

Some founders like to raise money from investors from Day 1 of their venture, but it's hard to raise money from investors just on the basis of a brilliant idea. Many people have brilliant ideas and until these ideas have been tested in the marketplace, they remain, well, only ideas and nothing more. So here are six things to have when building an entreprise that is ready for investors and to avoid the dreaded Outcome 3 of a zombie state.

Must-Have #1: The Audaciously Desirable Offering

High growth ventures that can exit in 36 months solve problems that are so big that their customers cannot stop talking about them to other potential customers. And they do so by offering a product or service that is so desirable that it can often look audacious when they first introduce it because no one has ever thought of it before. An audaciously desirable offering (ADO) carries a vision so appealing that customers have no choice but to agree and come on board with it.

And it doesn't stop there. Onboarded customers on board love the experience so much that they want to tell their friends about the product or service and are even willing to guide their friends in using it. It isn't easy to conceptualise such offerings and founders need to work hard and be extremely observant to notice the problems that their target customers desperately need solving. This challenge is compounded if our business operates within a crowded market with low profit margins. We then need to evaluate how to stand out from the competition in the Red Ocean to find a piece of Blue Ocean. In Chapter 3 "From Red to Blue", I discuss some ways to look at our businesses to help founders innovate a business plan, strategy and model in a crowded business environment.

In the end, the solutions we offer may not necessarily disrupt the status quo or change the business landscape where they operate, but they deliver a customer user experience that is so superior that nothing else comes close, at least for a while. They are characterised by some unique attributes which I will discuss in Chapter 2 "Present the Audaciously Desirable".

Must-Have #2: The Financial Targets and Dashboard

John P Kotter, in his book *Leading Change*,[1] states that an effective vision that moves people to act in alignment should be imaginable, desirable, feasible or attainable, focused, flexible and communicable. Concrete fiscal goals that are measurable give clarity to vision, and enable stakeholders to track progress, steer the enterprise, manage resources, and pivot the strategy where needed.

When framing the financial goals for a new venture, we should ask ourselves the following:

- What is the realistic market opportunity we can capture, based on the number of customers, and the price we can charge per customer in a year?
- What enterprise valuation do we hope to attain at the end of 36 months of incorporation?
- What evidence in the current market conditions suggests that we can ask for this enterprise valuation, if we can attain the financial goals we set?

When building up to these financial goals, we should never simply plug in numbers from assumptions that have little to no basis but we need to do a fair bit of research to see if what we say is valid and reasonable. For example, in determining the Total Addressable Market (TAM), it is often tempting to over-generalise the market we intend to operate in when our offering may only be attractive to a small subset of that market. As a result, the market sizing number can be so large that any derivation of market opportunity downstream will appear unrealistic.

Yes, we have all heard how some venture capitalists and startup accelerators would only invest in companies whose target market is at least US$1 billion or are able to show "explosive growth". I have met entrepreneurs who paid high fees to consultants to craft

---

1   John P Kotter, *Leading Change* (Boston: Harvard Business School Press, 1996).

an investment deck with insane market sizing and inflated financial projections because this is what they think is the way to convince top grade investors to consider investing in them. But let's be realistic: is that what the real world looks like? And if you put these astronomical numbers into the pitch deck, any savvy investor with an analyst on his payroll will dismiss your pitch narrative at first look. It makes you, as the founder, look really bad.

Then there is the question of revenue: how much revenue do we expect to achieve in 3, 6, 12, 24 and 36 months? How many customers would need to buy from us in order to reach those revenue numbers? Are the prices we set realistic?

As we project how the business will look numbers-wise, we will have a sense of whether our offering and business model is a scalable one that will attract investors or buyers in the foreseeable future. Beyond revenue, we need to track closely other indicators like Burn Multiple, Gross Profit Margins and EBITDA Margins, and be prepared to tweak the business model to scale it forward.

In Chapter 5 "Make Your Numbers Talk", I will discuss some of the financial indicators we need to pay attention to when growing our business and some of the pitfalls to avoid when sizing the market.

Numbers do tell a fair bit about our venture and how it is progressing. They do talk.

Must-Have #3: The Story

A great growth story does wonders for a new venture. It goes beyond simply presenting a compelling vision to detailing the attributes and design of the business that would make it possible to realise that vision. In building the growth story for a venture, founders need to be clear of the business model that can fetch the highest perceived value in the long term.

Some businesses are inherently scalable and therefore valuable to potential investors and buyers. It is thus vital to know what these businesses are and what makes them valuable. Knowing this will help founders to design more efficient enterprises that can take on more customers, deliver more value, and at less cost than their counterparts.

Founders also need to be clear about their venture's position in the market, and how it can avoid swimming in a crowded red ocean. The right position in the correct ecosystem could drastically reduce the friction for customers to come on board. The more coherently the pieces of the business come together, the better the story looks, and the more believable it is to potential investors.

In Chapter 4 "The Story of Our Business", I explore how some of the most prominent companies in the tech industry came head to head with each other and how some of the most rampantly useful tech products are no longer associated with the companies that invented them.

There may even exist pieces of gems in your own backyard that you haven't noticed before but could be that one thing that takes your business to a whole new level. If you can find such gems and build a compelling monetisation story around it, then the growth narrative for your enterprise could look a lot different from what it is now.

Must-Have #4: The Resource Hustle

Mention "resources needed to start a company" and fundraising often comes to the mind of new venture founders, but in this tough economic climate, investors will need evidence of early traction in revenue to suggest that customers may be keen to pay for the product or service. User counts alone may not cut it for the savvy investor, unless the startup is operating in a huge market with access to a phenomenally large number of users. Thus, founders may not have much choice but to bootstrap in the starting days of their ventures.

Beyond showing potential investors that they are serious about their business idea, founders who bootstrap in the starting phases of their ventures would prevent themselves from losing too much of their company early in the game. This is because equity is often priced the lowest at this stage of a venture.

When bootstrapping, founders should ask themselves this question: What is the lowest possible amount of money their venture will need to get the business off the ground to the point of generating revenue of up to $200,000 in three to five months?

But how do founders bootstrap when they are all too poor to buy new stuff or hire new people to even start? In Chapter 6 "Bootstrapping: Beg, Borrow, Build, Deal", I discuss the options available to new venture founders during the starting phases of an enterprise and how even industrial greats like Robert Iger, CEO of Disney, were able to get access to some super deals with Steve Jobs of Apple without spending a whole lot of money at the outset.

There are indeed cheap ways to get what we need to start things off.

Must-Have #5: The Lightning Push – Launching, Testing, Failing, Learning Really Fast

Hashim, who started an "OEM Meal" business, had no prior experience in the food business but always wanted to start one. We met over dinner and he shared with me how he first wanted to test if he could start a backend meal business in Singapore, preparing the type of food that hotels and catering companies would buy to serve their customers. He was aware that the operating costs for opening and running a big enough central kitchen in Singapore would be astronomical and could kill the business before it even got off the ground. Yet, he needed to start this quickly and learn fast on the job. He came up with a plan to survey all the central kitchens on the island and decided on one. Then he negotiated with the owner to lease the kitchen after hours at low cost, from late in the night until pre-dawn, to prepare the food for delivery at sunrise. He figured that this arrangement would help the central kitchen defray the cost of the premises during the day's downtime. Concurrently, by gaining access to the biggest expense item in the project at low cost, it would allow him to quickly launch his business, secure important revenue that would suggest that it is viable, learn quickly to tweak his product and service to the B2B customers, and gain the validation he needed to double down on a much bigger kitchen to serve a wider market. His business now includes some of the biggest hospital chains, hotels and catering companies as his clients.

When we get into the market to do the real selling, we need to get to the customer as quickly as possible, in as cheap a way as possible. We need to get the Minimum Viable Product (MVP) up in the shortest possible time and to avoid the "CAC Trap", where the Customer Acquisition Cost (CAC) is so high that it is almost impossible to make a profit from each sale.

There are indeed other ways to get one's product and message to the customer without having to spend a whole lot of money on paid advertising. And once the customer gets to experience the product, we need to keep checking to see if they love it enough to tell their friends about it. Doing all these quickly will help us learn fast to offer the market something that really sticks.

New ventures have short lifespans. They need to demonstrate the viability of the business narrative soon after launch or risk running itself into the ground. In Chapter 5 "Make Your Numbers Talk", I discuss the importance of bringing revenue in for the company early in the game and how we can do this creatively.

Must-Have #6: The Exit

As we build our venture into an enterprise and nurture its growth towards an exit, we will likely raise capital to fund the growth of the venture at some point. At the relevant point in time, depending on the stage of growth and how our enterprise is faring over different performance metrics that investors tend to look for, we may want to talk to some types of investors and not others. It makes sense to know that successfully raising capital isn't worth celebrating and having new investors on board can be a whole new challenge that founders may not be prepared for, as I will discuss in Chapter 9 "Raising Money for the First Time". Not all investments into a company are good for the founders, so it is crucial to know the difference.

Once we have built our enterprise to a level that potential buyers may take notice, it is time to prepare for an exit. It is tempting at this point to assume that the value of the enterprise may appreciate disproportionately under our continued leadership, but this assumption is more often flawed than accurate, especially for first time founders who are still learning on the job. So, the idea is to have a nice exit as soon as it is feasible to complete that Zero-to-One journey, to take home a decent sum of money from the transaction and start over with a new venture to solve a new problem.

The difference this time? We have the wisdom from our previous venture and the track record that will make our fundraising efforts a lot easier because we have proven to potential investors that we have done one full circle, from startup to exit.

In Chapter 10 "The Exit – Sell, Float or Close", I explore the reasoning behind an exit, even if it seems premature at first glance, and some options on how we can exit our enterprise, depending on its state at that point in time.

Know Your Numbers

One of the most brilliant investors I know once related to me his observation of what highly successful entrepreneurs – who grew their companies from a valuation of $1 million to $10 million, from $10 million to $100 million and from $100 million to $1 billion – have in common: they were either personally savvy or had someone who was finance savvy to help them. He reckoned that this often was a make-or-break factor for a growing enterprise.

This is no simple task for an entrepreneur, who already has the burden of charting a compelling vision for all stakeholders to believe that he or she can change the world with their business idea, and the responsibility of motivating the troops on the ground to fight until death to make this vision a reality. There is also a need to ensure that all the customers remain happy and stick around to buy more, subscribe further and spread the word to others. Already a jack of all trades, now the entrepreneur needs to double up as the CFO.

It all appears to be a tall order, but it can be manageable if one knows the right type of financial metrics to monitor and when to make the right decisions should the metrics swing one way or the other.

That is why an entrepreneur needs a financial dashboard to know what numbers to watch closely, and also a solid go-to-market playbook to know what marketing levers to pull that would not burn too much cash prematurely.

Enterprise valuation is a tricky thing and quite a different craft from what entrepreneurs are familiar with. But if the numbers check out nicely as one leads the team in this new venture, pitching the venture for investment or even an outright sale at a commendable valuation shouldn't be too herculean a task. One of the motivations behind writing Chapter 5 "Make Your Numbers Talk" is to help the number-illiterate founder find meaning in the financial indicators of his or her enterprise.

Plan and Navigate with Clarity

Most new ventures fail within 24 months of inception. With clarity of thought, target and thrust, we can mitigate this outcome. The 36-3 mandate for new ventures helps entrepreneurs ground their business ideation process and establishes a framework for building a business towards a vision of success that is imaginable, focused, concrete and compelling for all parties involved.

If we turn back to our initial discussion at the beginning of this chapter on AnalyzeEdu and LanguageStories, we can see that both companies may be heading for Outcome 3: the zombie state. So which company should pivot and which should double down on its current direction? And which aspects of each company's business should we be looking to change and build on? Where do we find the resources needed to effect these changes?

In the following chapters of this book, I will recall my own experience in running and exiting a few ventures, and call to mind the conversations I have had with successful entrepreneurs and seasoned investors as we explore the different facets of framing and growing a new venture and how these thoughts could potentially provide founders with insights on their businesses and possibly find new reasons to believe in what they have set out to do with their enterprises.

Let's start with the core of a successful venture: an ADO that delightfully solves a tremendous problem for its customers.

2

Present the Audaciously Desirable

Are the problems we are trying to solve big enough?

- Big enough for prospective customers to be beaming with delight when we show them what we can do for them;
- Big enough for customers to reach for their wallets and pay for our service the moment we pitch it to them;
- Big enough for them to tell their friends about us; and
- Big enough for their friends to rush to get our service?

How can we communicate to our customers that the solutions we offer can solve a problem so big that it would trigger such behaviour in them, even as they may not be aware of such a problem in the first place?

When dealing with bigger problems, conventional solutions that are already available will not do. Otherwise, the problems would not exist. Crafting a solution that can solve such problems demands deep domain expertise, a powerful imagination and a solid understanding of the customers' needs and pain points. The resulting solution may seem audacious to the customers at first glance but it becomes so desirable once they have used it.

> *An audaciously desirable offering is one that when it is first presented to the customer, promises an outcome so unlike what the customer has seen before that it would sound audacious, triggering a response that questions whether this offering is for real, or whether it can really deliver on such a promise. But once the use case is established and the market witnesses that it can deliver on what it promises, then the demand will take on a life of its own, promoting a unique combination of behavioural patterns.*

Let's discover more about these patterns of behaviour.

ADOs Trigger Unique Behavioural Patterns

Audaciously desirable offerings (ADOs) tend to promote the following patterns of behaviour from target customers or users:

- Our customers like to talk about us to their friends;
- Our competitors laugh at us, then play copycat;
- The media catches on quickly;
- The FOMO effect; and
- We are fans.

ADO Behaviour #1: Our Customers Talk about Us

"Have you tried ChatGPT yet?" This was the first thing my friend, whom I had not spoken to for months, said to me when we met recently. Since its release in November 2022, ChatGPT has been the talk of the town. Many of us have used it and some have questioned its impact on learning, while others are eagerly anticipating if Google will have a response to it, but mostly, people whom I have met who have tried ChatGPT have told me what they used it for and how they used it, as I have done so, too. ChatGPT's ability seemed so audacious when we first heard about it. But when we see what it can really do, it becomes so desirable. And we cannot stop talking about it.

If our offering to the market is audaciously desirable, our users will talk about us.

So how do we find out if our users are talking about our product or even promoting it to their friends? One quick way is by checking the Net Promoter Score (NPS). An NPS of greater than 8.5 suggests that our offering is awesome enough for our users to tell others about us. And we need to keep finding ways to engage with our customers to see if there are things we need to change, experiences we need to elevate, to the point where they cannot stop talking about us to their friends. It is only through such intimate understanding and a relentless desire to care for our customers that will yield insights on just what they really need, and not just what they think they need. I will discuss further the use of NPS in Chapter 8 "Going to Market".

ADO Behaviour #2: Our Competitors Laugh at Us, then Copy Us

For years the automobile industry has been dominated by a few main players as a result of consolidation from some 200 car makers in the 1920s.[2] For decades, gasoline-powered vehicles were practically the only engine choice available to the customer and automakers fought hard in branding and marketing to get their vehicles out of the showrooms. Buying a car would involve numerous trips to different showrooms, test driving different vehicles, accompanied by long-drawn sessions with the salesperson.

Then came Tesla, whose battery-powered cars have revolutionised the car industry and created a whole new market for electric vehicles (EVs).

Tesla pioneered the narrative of a green vehicle, which is an oxymoron since prior to the advent of the EV, internal combustion vehicles have been blamed as one of the main culprits for global warming and climate change.

2   Lou Shipley, "How Tesla Sets Itself Apart" *Harvard Business Review* (28 February 2020) <https://hbr.org/2020/02/how-tesla-sets-itself-apart>.

Today, almost all major automakers have an electric vehicle in their catalogue or have serious plans for building one.

But it didn't start off like this. When Tesla first emerged to challenge the automotive industry, it was laughed at by its competitors, some even calling it a joke that came out of Silicon Valley. For example, according to the *Los Angeles Times*, Daimler's former chairman Edzard Reuter had, in November 2015, called Elon Musk, the founder of Tesla, "a pretender" and commented that Tesla couldn't be taken seriously compared to its dominant automaker peers in Germany.[3] Bob Lutz, former vice chairman of General Motors and Chrysler, said in September 2018 that Musk didn't know how to run a car company and predicted that Tesla was "headed for the graveyard".[4]

When we present an ADO to the market, our competitors tend to laugh off what we are proposing to achieve for our customers. "Can they even make money out of this product?", "They have got to be joking!", "What do they know about this industry that makes them qualified to make such a claim?!", "We will finish them off in a heartbeat!" – these are just some of the comments and rhetoric we can expect from our competitors, especially the well-entrenched ones. So, if we hear such comments from our competitors, then it suggests that we may be on to something so audacious that they don't think it's doable. And it is up to us to prove them wrong.

Here's the thing: once we can deliver on the promises we make on our ADO, we would have successfully reshaped the competition, possibly setting a new standard, a new way of doing things, elevating the customer experience to a whole new level.

Then something else starts to happen: our competitors will start emulating us, offering similar services, imitating us.

When we reach a certain level of traction in a short period of time (within 18 months or less), two groups of people may take notice:

3   Erik Kirschbaum, "German automakers who once laughed off Elon Musk are now starting to worry" *Los Angeles Times* (19 April 2016) <https://www.latimes.com/business/autos/la-fi-hy-0419-tesla-germany-20160419-story.html>.

4   "Are There Any Automakers That Can Rival Tesla?" Electric Car FAQ (7 July 2020) <https://sites.google.com/site/electriccarsfaq/tesla/arethereanyautomakersthatcanrivaltesla>.

- The current players in the market, who would be wondering if we are onto something sustainable that they can do with the resources they have on hand and drown us out before we get any further, or start a conversation with us to discuss collaborations, partnerships, some form of investment into our enterprise, or to learn about how we do it with the intention to copy (I have seen a fair bit of this last part in the past few years, so founders beware).

- People on the sidelines, watching how we have grown so quickly and wondering if it's time to jump in and take a slice of what we have achieved. Many of them are aspiring startup founders, or our suppliers/partners, who believe that they can do a much better job, or at the very least make a quick entry into the market to dilute our share of it, since we have started not too long ago and have already achieved that much success, which would suggest that the barrier to entry is quite low.

At this point, it is important to audit our position and what makes our offering so sticky with our customers. Crucially, we need to review if our current customer base is protectable and what we need to do to stay ahead of the pack. For example, in some jurisdictions, government contracts rarely span more than two years with the same vendor, which poses a risk if the bulk of our revenue is derived from such contracts in a single territory, and we should appreciate that customers are rarely loyal to vendors. In many instances, we may need to consider doing things that will disrupt the current state that we have established.

ADO Behaviour #3: The Mass Media Catches On

Amazon has a practice whenever a new product is being designed for the market: the team would first draft an internal press release to announce the finished product.[5] That's even before the product is built! This process, known as "working backwards", places the

---

5   Justin Bariso, "Amazon Has a Secret Weapon Known as 'Working Backwards' – and It will Transform the Way You Work" Inc. (16 December 2019) <https://www.inc.com/justin-bariso/amazon-uses-a-secret-process-for-launching-new-ideas-and-it-can-transform-way-you-work.html>.

focus on the customer, the problems he or she is facing, and how the envisioned product could convincingly solve those problems. If the product narrative in the press release isn't compelling enough, the product manager would need to go back to the drawing board and reiterate, until it gets the nod to be built, or gets the order to be killed.

ADOs are often novel and inspiring, the type that reporters and journalists like to write about. These offerings solve old problems in new ways that others have not thought were possible. And those who can do it shine as a beacon for the rest to look up to, to emulate, to learn from. This is especially true for a consumer-facing offering and the challenge of the founder is to apply the knowledge of customers' problems and to constantly design solutions that catch the attention of the media to write about them as news or insights to share. It's no easy task but founders should constantly test their product vision and the impact on society against whether such impact could get to a larger audience through the news media, for the right reasons, of course.

In Chapter 8 "Going to Market", I will discuss how we can frame our offering in a manner that attracts the attention of the mass media.

ADO Behaviour #4: The Sticky and FOMO Effect

"My wife would spend days filling her shopping cart. And at the stroke of midnight on the 11th of November, she would place all the orders. By then, I would be fast asleep." A friend of mine related to me the "11.11" shopping phenomenon – otherwise known as "Singles Day", the 11.11 event was started by Alibaba in 2009 to boost purchases at its online marketplace, Taobao. Since then, it has become a cultural phenomenon in China that has spread to many parts of Asia, where people would expect steep discounts from merchants for only a limited amount of time and stock. The sense of scarcity promoted by this event has created the FOMO effect.

The fear of missing out (FOMO) relates to a basic aspect of human nature as most of us don't like to lose out to others. Once a product or service catches on and customers start telling their friends about it, the phone will start to ring and we may start getting enquiries on LinkedIn or through our website. And when our capacity to service all interested customers is limited, the FOMO effect kicks in.

Once our customers sign on to use our product or service, they can't seem to get enough of it. This is the concept of being "sticky". It is important, however, to distinguish being sticky from being addictive. For one, a sticky product does not necessarily cause the user to engage with it at every waking moment. That is what an addictive product does. While many addictive products could turn out to be ADOs, I do not think that all ADOs need to be addictive for the user. In fact, I would argue that addictive ADOs may often face backlash from certain user groups and if their scale isn't big enough, they could face being disrupted by lobbyists, by the authorities or by competitors.

A sticky offering is different. It causes a top-of-mind effect in the customer. It means that whenever our customer wants to get a specific job done and our product is able to do that job, the customer would only consider our product as the first choice amongst all other competing products. This doesn't need to happen at every moment of the customer's life, not even daily or weekly. But our offering needs to be the customer's go-to-source whenever the demand for it arises.

And when our offering has such a sticky effect on our customers and is in limited supply, FOMO will kick in even more.

If our customers behave in this way, it would suggest that we may be on to a compelling product or service that is highly desirable.

Often, this is when problems may arise to break a company. When a company is overwhelmed by its customers' requests and is unable to provide a solid customer experience with its service, then the successes it has gained with the ADO can quickly disappear. It is tempting for the founder to take on as many deals as they come, but it can turn out to be a grave mistake if the enterprise is unable to service its customers in the right way. As quickly as the good word that our customers put out for us when they first experienced our product or service, these same customers can also kill us with bad reviews.

So, it is important to stay centred on the customer, to ensure that each one is treated in the best way we see possible according to the promises of our product. Once we start seeing our ADO traction build up, we need to evaluate if our business backend and structure is built to enable us to scale up, to take in lots of customers without incurring excessive cost and time to service them. Just as important, when things don't work out and our customers feel short-changed, we need to ensure that our efforts in customer recovery are so impressive that we will not lose a customer but will gain a loyal evangelist for our work. I will discuss more on this aspect in Chapter 7 "Know Your Customer, Love Your Customer".

ADO Behaviour #5: You Want to Use it Yourself, as Often as You Can

On many weekends, some years back, my lunch would consist of just one dish: fish soup with rice from a food centre in the middle of town. This was not some cool and comfortable location with nice seating within walking distance from my home. Far from it – I would drive 30 minutes to the food centre just to have that same meal. Once there, I would queue for at least 45 minutes to place my order, and the stall owners were not the friendliest sort (they would rudely disallow customers from taking an extra clean bowl to share their dish and would be impatient when customers were not crystal clear with their orders). And it wasn't cheap. Based on a recipe that spanned two generations, a typical dish could cost three times that of a main course from another stall in the same place. Yet, fans of this dish would queue quietly, patiently, meekly, just to savour it. Clearly the product was excellent.

Here is something I noticed: the cooks ate only what they cooked for their customers and they would do this practically every day. I figured that it was not likely to save cost, since the raw ingredients for the dish they served wasn't cheap. Yet, they couldn't think of eating anything else. Imagine doing that every day and not getting bored with it.

Do you have the same belief in your offering? This is not quite the same as testing the product to see if the user experience is "good enough", but it stems from a genuine appreciation of the value of the product to solve a problem that affects common folks such as yourself or your family members. If you who have created the product do not feel drawn to use it frequently, then you shouldn't expect others to do so.

ADOs have Unique Attributes

Having spoken to numerous innovative entrepreneurs, and having observed how some products and marketing campaigns are able to trigger almost illogical responses from customers to want them, I have noted that ADOs have the following attributes:

- They deliver a great deal for the customer;
- They present a vision like no other to their users;
- They command a price premium that is way higher than the industry average;
- They deliver disproportionately better results than their competitors;
- They deliver what the customers want, not just what they need; and
- They aren't necessarily epic and can be temporary.

A Good Deal can be an ADO, for a Short While

When I was nine years old, I started my first venture. At that time, a certain probiotic drink had a great campaign that offered one scratch card featuring a cartoon character with every bottle purchased, with each bottle costing 40 cents. The scratch cards could reveal some small prizes, but most of the time, we had to contend with "Try Again!". It may not seem like much by today's standards, but in those days, this offer was riveting and my schoolmates and I would save up to buy as many bottles of the drink as we could, just to get those cards to complete our collection (there were many characters to collect).

Some of us would down as many as four to five bottles a day – a great detoxification exercise, no less. And every day, I would go to the store near my home to buy even more bottles with whatever money I had left for the day. Then one day, the curious store owner asked me, "Boy, why do you keep buying so many bottles of this drink every day?".

"Because I want to get the (scratch) card," I replied. The conversation that followed primed my first venture.

Store owner: "If the card is what you want, I can sell you the card and you don't have to buy each bottle of drink for 40 cents."

"How much will you charge for each card?"

"Ten cents per card."

Credit should go to the store owner for offering me this deal to buy those cartoon character scratch cards directly from him, as I would not have thought of making such an inquiry, let alone figuring out this "direct-to-supplier" strategy at that age.

"Yet, chance favours only the prepared mind," said the iconic microbiologist and chemist, Louis Pasteur, in 1854. A mind on the lookout to solve a problem is more likely to notice when the solution presents itself, while a curious heart and a willing hand may just be enough to take on the solution to change the world with a problem requiring this very solution. I like to think that I had a prepared mind back then, because the next thing I did was to empty my wallet of the $2 that I had and bought 20 cards.

I didn't scratch any of them but brought them all to school the next day. I used the same argument on my friends and within ten minutes, I had exhausted my stock and made $4. I went back to the store and bought 40 cards, did the same thing and repeated the cycle for a whole three months. Word started to spread and students from other classes came looking for me to buy cards from my stock each day. In the end, I made enough money to buy my entire Star Wars toy collection, which I have kept until today.

Consumers are generally drawn to a good deal. That's why many are drawn to special offers, sales campaigns that offer up to 70 per cent discount on some items on a particular day, extra "bonus" loyalty points, free shipment, etc, and the list goes on. eCommerce players are highly skilled at playing up such behaviour through campaigns that offer steep discounts off some items on specific days, such as the "Black Friday Sale" in the US and the 11.11 or Singles Day sale, which was started in China by Taobao and progressively radiated to other eCommerce providers in Asia. In such campaigns where stocks on offer are limited, we can see the FOMO effect kicking in. Thus, if you can deliver a great deal to your customers, you may be on to something desirable for them. But be aware that FOMO is often temporary and it is wise not to depend on just this singular pattern of behaviour to anchor the offering. Therefore, to really hook the target customer with an ADO, you may need something more.

So how can we find and present the audaciously desirable vision of success to our customers to solve problems that really matter to them? We don't need to look much further than Steve Jobs and his unveiling of Apple's first iPod.

ADOs are Premised on a Vision that is Compelling like No Other

When Apple's Steve Jobs introduced the first iPod, his iconic slogan was simply, "1,000 songs in your pocket."

It wasn't about the features of the device, its dimensions or how people will be thrilled to use it in different ways. No. That slogan summed up the vision of what the device was designed to do and created the space for so much more imagination by its owner when he or she got their hands on it.

I understood this when I started an education company in 2000. It was my second venture (the first being the one I started at the age of 9). In 2000 and the few years that followed, this company offered enrichment programmes to students in Singapore schools. But I wasn't the first to do this there. There were already players in the market offering similar services to schools and this gave me reason to believe that there was money to be made from this business. But I didn't think that the existing offerings were attractive enough to make a sustainable business and I needed to dig deep and find out just what sort of vision I could propose to school leaders that would excite them to tell others about us, and if this vision would garner media attention (novelty). Crucially, the vision needed to touch the hearts of educators and inspire them to let their students learn a new craft that could change the world.

I figured that we could expose our students to the world of life and environmental sciences, the stuff that COVID-19 vaccine, lab-cultured meat, climate change and paternity testing were based on.

We were pioneers in this field, helping students in primary and secondary schools understand complex concepts that their school teachers had learned in university. Understandably, many of the educators whom I met laughed at what I was proposing and turned me down.

But I didn't give up. I reviewed each criticism to sieve out the aspects of my proposal that turned them away, then refined the offering, pitched to the next educator on my list and repeated the process. This went on a few times, before I met an enlightened school leader, who requested that I share my entire proposal in just five sentences so she could grasp how big a deal this was. I did just that. Then she took out her school calendar and offered me my first major deal: to equip more than 50 per cent of her students with the knowledge, skills and exposure to this whole new world as she recognised them as essential foundations for her students, even if they did not intend to pursue a career in STEM (Science, Technology, Engineering and Mathematics). We collaborated and before long, the newspapers heard about it and wanted to do a piece on the school with us as enablers, and in November that year, we hit the major newsreels big time.

After the initial period of scepticism, the life sciences education movement caught on and our phones kept ringing without us having to make any more cold calls. Due to our limited capacity, we had to turn away customers, and this led to more customers rushing to sign on with us in an upward virtuous spiral. The startup's revenue increased by more than 20 times within a 24-month period and our staff headcount went from two to 30 during that time. This might not be much in large markets, but in a small market like Singapore, it was something significant.

Some years later, I had the opportunity to ask two of the school leaders who were the first to jump onto our offering, just what made them believe in a startup like mine that no one had heard of before. They revealed that I had presented a vision that was so compelling to them, and a playbook that was so systematic that they had nothing else to question me on but to go on this ride with me.

An ADO stems from a vision that is so compelling that users have no choice but to try it for themselves. And if this offering delivers on its promises, people will hear about it and news will spread quickly.

Finding that vision and use case narrative, and being able to communicate it in a highly concise manner is crucial. In startup pitching to investors, founders are expected to be able to communicate their startup businesses to potential investors while sharing the same elevator with them – this is commonly called the elevator pitch. The same is demanded here: convey and convince with clarity in five sentences what the big deal is about your offering that the customer must sign on with you, and you may be on to a tsunami of deals.

ADOs are Priced Way Higher than Their Peers

When the iPhone was first introduced, it was priced much higher than a typical smartphone at that time, when users of mobile phones didn't want to pay a lot for a phone (see table below). It also lacked several features expected in a mobile phone then, but that did not stop consumers from getting their hands on the product. In fact, many observers at that time noted the overnight queues forming at Apple stores prior to the release of the first iPhone, and subsequent releases that similarly drew long lines of customers.[6]

6   Lisa Eadicicco, "This is Why the iPhone Upended the Tech Industry" *Time* (29 June 2017) <https://time.com/4837176/iphone-10th-anniversary/>.

Device	Average Price (2007)
iPhone (8GB)	$499 (2-year AT&T contract signed separately)[7]
BlackBerry 8800	From $299[8] on a two-year contract
Palm Treo 750	$399[9] on a two-year contract
Nokia E62	$199[10] on a two-year contract
T-Mobile G1 (runs on Android)	$150 on a two-year contract

In the same way, when we launched our life sciences learning programme in local schools, the fees we charged were easily two to three times those that our competitors were charging. Despite the higher fees, our clients returned each year to renew their contract with us, some even for five to ten years. So, what gave us the qualification to charge such significantly higher fees when we were largely offering similar services to our competitors?

When a product or service is able to wow its customers and trigger audaciously desirable behavioural patterns, customers tend to be more tolerant of higher prices to justify the perceived value, which they do not see in comparable products. But these customers are not just paying to use the product but are actually paying for a much more comprehensive experience that is provided by the vendor. It is these peripheral experiences that are integral to the core offering which makes it so desirable that customers are willing to pay more and keep returning each year. In the later chapters, I will discuss the importance of providing a total customer experience in an ADO.

7   Kyle Mickalowski, Mark Mickelson & Jaciel Keltgen, "Apple's iPhone Launch: A Case Study in Effective Marketing" (2008) 9(2) The Business Review 283 <https://www.augie.edu/sites/default/files/u57/pdf/jaciel_subdocs/iPhone.pdf>.

8   Bonnie Cha, "BlackBerry 8800" CNET (22 May 2007) <https://www.cnet.com/reviews/blackberry-8800-review/>.

9   Ryan Block, "Palm Treo 750 launch presentation, including price and release date" Engadget (4 January 2007) <Palm Treo 750 launch presentation, including price and release date | Engadget)>.

10   Ryan Block, "Nokia E62 to drop for $299/$199 in September/October" Engadget (28 June 2006) <https://sg.news.yahoo.com/2006-06-27-nokia-e62-to-drop-for-599-399-in-september-october.html?guccounter=1&guce_referrer=aHR0cHM6Ly93d3cuZ29vZ2xlLmNvbVS88&guce_referrer_sig=AQAAAFalTDMBHynai9a4_5fRqeCF219aILAmMCH3n9Fb9RWXVLSdfhhkxAkD3r1nstzPe3WbfYPLVKj6aQfCozjSzqWs9ddaH7v9rNBjy1z2VrN7m8GxiS57l93D-QNdG0y4WlSqtB1kP-EhRA-rJn4gIN7Y243ioBW9xbC3OepHjU8QQ>.

ADOs Deliver Disproportionate Results

ChatGPT, the AI-driven conversational tool developed by OpenAI, has been used by millions since its launch in November 2022. At its core is its ability to serve as a search engine and reply in text form to a user's query, although there are limitations to its accuracy and breadth of coverage beyond what it is trained to do. This is where ChatGPT is such a desirable tool: what would normally take a researcher many hours to search online can be compiled by ChatGPT and represented even in a table format in a matter of seconds. This disproportionately efficient output by the AI tool was audacious when we first heard about it; when we tried it and saw that it worked, it soon became an indispensable tool for many.

(Qualification: while ChatGPT has had many use cases, I do not recommend taking its output wholesale without doing sufficient fact checking. In fact, ChatGPT itself has said that it uses its language generation capabilities to generate a response based on the input it was trained on, which may not always be accurate or up-to-date).

The education company I had founded in 2000 for life sciences education had, by 2006, pioneered another product offering in the form of a new way of blended teaching. In this offering, teachers would use a set of interactive teaching resources that would guide them to deliver superior learning experiences and outcomes for students, regardless of their skills level. We wanted to solve an age-old problem faced by ministries of education worldwide, of not being able to deliver consistently good education outcomes because of the diverse teaching abilities of their educators. Governments worldwide that have invested heavily in teacher professional development have also met with limited success.

We figured out a way to crack this and we proposed a bold narrative for an institutionalised method of instruction that would enable all teachers to attain a basal level of teaching standards in the classroom, regardless of their starting point. While it may not have been able to deliver a personalised learning experience and pathway for students that a world class education system is expected to provide, it would help governments that were struggling with uneven standards to level up everyone in a short time and pave the way for refinement later on to meet even better outcomes. Having succeeded with this model in an earlier venture within the company, we boldly stepped out of our home market in Singapore and went to pitch to the Director-General of the Ministry of Education in a neighbouring country.

This would turn out to be my third venture – on blended teaching.

I remember vividly how that meeting went. It was near the end of the work day when the Director-General for Education (DGE) and his colleague met my team. After my presentation and pitch, he leaned back in his seat and made just two remarks and asked one question:

The Question: "Mr Eric, are you aware that we have more teachers in our country than you have students in yours?"

The Remarks: "Yet you have come here to ask us to believe you when we have invested millions into e-learning and the results are still dismal to say the least. I'm sure we are not doing something right but I just don't know what it is."

At that moment, I felt that the only way to convince him and his colleague was to show him how it would work in his schools. So I took the opportunity to ask him for two things:

- To allow me to pilot our solution in any school of his choice to prove that what we have presented works; and
- To let us hack into and modify some of the teaching content packages that they have paid millions to produce and show them how small adjustments can change the whole dynamics of learning, and also to prove that we knew what we were doing.

"So, you wish to prove on our land that your method works?" He asked again, before agreeing to my requests.

The DGE gave us two rural schools to prove our worth: one deep in the forest and another on a scenic mountain. For nine months, we let the teachers use our learning content package and the one we modified with their MOE's permission. After nine months of this pilot project, the MOE assessed the students' performance through two independently set tests that they had commissioned the nation's teaching college to administer.

The results: the students recorded on average an improvement in scores of more than 200 per cent, from an average score of 30 to scoring an average of 70 points out of 100.

This was something not foreseen by the MOE. And coming from rural schoolchildren, the impact of this improvement was even more dramatic. The DGE was so pleasantly surprised that he summoned the top management of the MOE to visit these schools to see just what was done differently that created this marked improvement in the schools.

On the business side, this successful pilot paved the way for a substantial order from the MOE for our product. Just as important, many teachers' lives were changed for the better as a result of adopting this solution for their classrooms.

When a solution initially seems like a misfit on first glance but delivers an impact that is so pronounced that it shifts paradigms, it is an ADO. It delivers disproportionately better results than its closest competitors.

A disproportionately better result is not one that is incrementally better than a comparable product or service, but one that exceeds the expectations of its users to a level that they have not thought possible.

It does that by changing the rules of the game.

The iPhone did that by providing a handheld computer in our hands and the internet at our fingertips – the mobile phone would never look the same again.

ADOs Deliver What Users Want

"We only invest in companies that offer products and services that are 'must-haves' and not 'good-to-have'", quipped one venture capitalist when asked about his investment strategy.

Yet, for all things, there are two kinds of "must-haves" for the customer: what I need and what I want.

In 2000, Macdonald's in Singapore launched a Hello Kitty toy promotion that involved giving away limited edition Hello Kitty stuffed toys with purchases of selected menu items. The promotion caused a frenzy among customers, leading to long lines, outlets that were sold out of the toys and fights among customers were often seen at these outlets. Some customers even bought menu items they didn't want just to get their hands on the popular toys. Others resorted to buying the toys at sky-high prices from those who managed to get it at the outlets, creating a thriving and almost unreal secondary market. This promotion is still remembered today as one of the most iconic marketing campaigns by McDonald's in Singapore.

So, based on the customers' behaviour, would the Hello Kitty stuffed toys be considered a "must-have"?

Yet, wouldn't these toys be a "want" and not a "need"?

As we can see in this Macdonald's Hello Kitty example, while a "want" may not stem from a physiological need in Maslow's hierarchy, we can argue that people may sacrifice what they need in order to get what they want in life.

So, when we deliver to our customers what they want, we will invariably trigger a behaviour that is uniquely associated with an ADO.

ADOs May Not be Epic and Can be Temporary

Just because a product or service can produce phenomenal results and trigger a user response unlike others doesn't mean that it requires incredible budgets to power, nor is it always a result of years of research and development, incurring high levels of financial investment and risk. In fact, an ADO may not even be protectable and may be prone to competition over time. This is because if an offering is so awesome, competitors will certainly take notice and want to jump in to take a bite of the market share that this offering has gained in a short period of time. And very soon, a blue ocean can become a red ocean (more on this in the following chapter).

We have seen this in many instances, from the Android smartphone challenging the Apple iPhone, to copycat service providers entering the market to dilute our market share in education enrichment, to more efficient players offering a smoother service that can disrupt incumbent providers.

Any traction that an ADO has built up can be diluted in a matter of a few years, and in some markets, in a matter of months. It is thus imperative that a founder continuously finds inspiration to stay ahead of the pack, to offer something yet more desirable when others are just playing catch up. Also, as will be discussed in subsequent chapters, an ADO that is more protectable is seldom confined to just one product or service but usually comprises several components working together to realise a compelling vision that is orchestrated by a superior and able team. The more integrated an ADO is with other peripheral services, the more likely its position in the market will be protected. And the more capable the team behind it, the higher the chance of innovating and presenting another ADO soon after.

So, what can founders do to innovate and design offerings that may emerge as audaciously desirable to the customer?

The following are five things to start with.

Five Things to Do to Envision the Audaciously Desirable
#1: Don't Ask the Customer

Walter Isaacson, in his biography of Steve Jobs, summarised Jobs' view of imagining the audaciously desirable for the customer.[11] Here is an excerpt:

> When Jobs took his original Macintosh team on its first retreat, one member asked whether they should do some market research to see what customers wanted.

---

11   Walter Isaacson, "The Real Leadership Lessons of Steve Jobs" *Harvard Business Review* (April 2012) <https://hbr.org/2012/04/the-real-leadership-lessons-of-steve-jobs>.

"No," Jobs replied, "because customers don't know what they want until we've shown them." He invoked Henry Ford's line "If I'd asked customers what they wanted, they would have told me, 'A faster horse!'"

Caring deeply about what customers want is much different from continually asking them what they want; it requires intuition and instinct about desires that have not yet formed. "Our task is to read things that are not yet on the page," Jobs explained. Instead of relying on market research, he honed his version of empathy—an intimate intuition about the desires of his customers. He developed his appreciation for intuition—feelings that are based on accumulated experiential wisdom— while he was studying Buddhism in India as a college dropout.

Quite often, our customers are not in a position to tell us just what will wow them into buying from us, and we need to dig deep to study the market, the players in the market, their daily actions, the problems they are facing, the aspirations they have for the work they are doing. Going to the customer and asking for them to give us directions may not be the most effective way, as observed by Henry Ford. We need to "read things that are not yet on the page", and to develop "an intimate intuition about the desires of [the customer]", as Steve Jobs had put it.

So, how can we develop such intuition? One way is to pay close attention to the customer.

#2: Observe the Customer Closely
In his review of Japanese carmaker, Honda, Jeffrey Rothfeder[12] noted "the group's emphasis that knowledge has to be acquired first hand – called *sangen shugi*." He observed and figured that this was "the reason why Honda engineers can still be found hanging around car parks

---

12   Andrew Hill, "'Driving Honda' by Jeffrey Rothfeder" *Financial Times* (26 July 2014) <https://www.ft.com/content/d48af06c-11ba-11e4-a17a-00144feabdc0>.

watching people load and unload their vehicles as they look for hints about how to refine the company's first North American truck."

In user experience studies, a UX designer would often observe and take notes of selected customers as they navigate through a website or an app. The UX designer may not interact with the customer much during the process, except to occasionally ask questions surrounding the thinking behind some actions. In particular, the designer would pay attention to where the customer would get stuck in the process, to find out just how to improve on the user experience.

This isn't the easiest thing for a business owner and entrepreneur to do. As the ones who have conceptualised the product and led the discussion on positioning and workflow, it takes a whole lot of humility to see how our design can fall apart in the hands of a user. It is easier to ask an employee to do these things, but if the product owner does not care enough about the customer, then how can he inspire his team to do the same?

The importance of closely observing the ground where the action takes place cannot be overemphasised. Business, by nature, is a social process. People make decisions, and decisions affect how a business operates. The more we know about the people we are targeting and the decisions they make on a daily basis, the more insights we will have on what we can do to help them along.

When observing our prospects, we need to take note of their habits and the subtle nuances they display when going about their business. Then we need to take all these cues and put together a narrative against the jobs that they need to get done on a daily basis. Most importantly, we need to pay close attention to the workarounds and the "hoops" they need to jump over to get these jobs done. This will reveal their pain points and give us a sense of where current offerings fall short, which opens a window for innovations to happen. The more inefficient the process in our target market, the greater the opportunity for innovation. And if you are the one who can innovate to deliver something that radically elevates the way the same job is done by the customer, you may have an ADO in hand. In the next chapter, I will discuss how we can use this thinking to analyse a crowded market and find a breakthrough.

#3: Find Inspiration Elsewhere

Just as we look for other places to deploy our product or service concepts, it is also helpful to pay attention to what others are doing in their industries and wonder if those practices or business models could work in our business. I use the word "wonder" because we wouldn't know if there is a fit until we go in deeper to study the finer elements of those business models and evaluate if they could be tweaked to help us solve our customers' problems. Wai Fong Boh and Thara Ravindran advocated that the practice of emulating business practices from other industries can be a powerful way to identify business opportunities and possibly design business models and customer experiences that could set us apart from our competitors.[13]

One example of how a company has been able to adopt practices in another industry to become a market leader in its own industry is Tesla in the automotive industry. Unlike other automakers, Tesla builds its software on the car's hardware, much like the way software and computer companies build their products. This design and development approach fundamentally challenges the conventional way which other car companies build their cars and enables Tesla to constantly improve on the software every few weeks as compared to other car companies, which do not update the software in their cars throughout the lifetime of the vehicle.[14]

Tesla also adopts the approach of how computer companies sell their products: customers view different models online, make the choice for features, pay the deposit and schedule the pickup, much like how we would buy an iPhone from Apple or laptop from Dell. This direct-to-consumer approach bypasses the middlemen, the

---

13 Wai Fong Boh & Thara Ravindran, *Identifying Business Opportunities Through Innovation* (World Scientific, 2023).

14 Lou Shipley, "How Tesla Sets Itself Apart" *Harvard Business Review* (28 February 2020) <https://hbr.org/2020/02/how-tesla-sets-itself-apart>.

distributors that practically all car companies use when they enter any market. As a result, the profit margin for each vehicle sold by Tesla is much higher than that of other brands. In the third quarter of 2022, the gross profit per vehicle sold by Tesla is more than twice that of a Volkswagen, four times higher than a Toyota and five times higher than a Ford in a comparable category.[15]

Having high gross profit margins is crucial to helping a company scale, as I will elaborate in Chapter 5 "Make Your Numbers Talk".

#4: Extend Your Competencies to Other Products

The private hire cab driver who recently ferried me from home to office couldn't stop talking about how great his electric car was performing against its petrol counterparts. The acceleration, the smoothness of the drive, the ease and significantly lower cost of maintenance … he went on and on. And at the end of the ride, I was almost sold to visit the car showroom to check out this car. When a customer sells your product like this at no benefit to himself whatsoever, you know that this product is an ADO.

This was not a Tesla. This car was a BYD from China.

And BYD (an acronym for "Build Your Dreams") didn't start off building cars like Tesla did. Wang Chuan-Fu founded BYD in 1995 as a manufacturer of rechargeable batteries for mobile phones. And by 2000, it was already supplying to Motorola and Nokia, swiftly becoming one of the world's largest rechargeable batteries manufacturers.[16] It only started getting into the automaker business in 2002, as a car manufacturer in China. One of BYD's strengths has been its ability to make the manufacturing process highly efficient and productive. And this resulted in higher profits than their peers in the same industry and lower prices to customers.[17]

15 Paul Lienert & Joseph White, "Analysis: Tesla uses its profits as a weapon in an EV price war" Reuters (20 January 2023) <https://www.reuters.com/business/autos-transportation/tesla-uses-its-profits-weapon-in-an-ev-price-war-2023-01-19/>.

16 Marc Gunther, "Warren Buffett takes charge" *Fortune Magazine* (13 April 2009) <https://money.cnn.com/2009/04/13/technology/gunther_electric.fortune/>.

17 "China's BYD is overtaking Tesla as the carmaker extraordinaire" *The Economist* (2 February 2023) <https://www.economist.com/business/2023/02/02/chinas-byd-is-overtaking-tesla-as-the-carmaker-extraordinaire>.

There is one other strategy that stood out for BYD: as a newcomer to the EV industry, BYD leveraged on their ability to create lower-priced EVs and focused on undeveloped EV markets. As the manufacturer of EVs for plebeians, BYD looks poised to emerge as a leader in this space, possibly selling more cars than any of its peers.

In the next chapter, I explore how we can analyse our core competencies to derive offerings that can help us out-compete our peers in a crowded market.

#5: Find the Silver Lining – Looking in the Wrong Place with Your Solution

In the late 1980s, two British scientists created a drug that they believed could be used to treat high blood pressure and angina, a chest pain associated with coronary heart disease. A patent was subsequently filed for it as heart medication. In the early 1990s, a famous drug company conducted several clinical trials of the drug, only to find that it wasn't that effective as a treatment for heart disease. But something else happened: a certain vital organ in male subjects was observed to be highly active for several days after taking the drug. The drug company then pivoted the trials to focus on using the drug to correct erectile dysfunction, and filed a patent for the drug as treatment for this condition, which the US FDA approved in March 1998.[18]

We now know that the drug company was Pfizer, and the experimental drug would become known as Viagra, or some colloquially refer to as "the blue pill".

Although the condition is not quite as life threatening as heart disease, it is no less severe in many ways for those who suffer from it. And if the scientists had not looked hard enough at the data, they might not have discovered the efficacious use of Viagra that has changed the lives of millions of people.

Quite often, we find ourselves in a dilemma: our product doesn't seem to sell well enough for us to call it a winner, nor does it flop

---

18   Jacque Wilson, "Viagra: The little blue pill that could" CNN (27 March 2013) <https://edition. cnn.com/2013/03/27/health/viagra-anniversary-timeline/index.html#:~:text=Take%20a%20 look%20back%20at,is%20classified%20as%20UK%2D92480>.

sufficiently for us to call it a failure. But if we look hard enough at the data, and think hard enough about what it means, perhaps we can find something that suggests that this solution may just work in another setting, to some other customers, for a totally different purpose. I challenge founders and business owners, especially those of us who are stuck, to dig deep, think laterally and pan your view to find that audaciously desirable narrative for a new customer, to meet a new need, in an awesome way.

Humility, Honesty and a Lot of Imagination to Find the Audaciously Desirable

Framing an audaciously desirable narrative is essentially branding and product development at its core. More importantly, it forces us to think deeply about whether there is really a big enough problem to be solved in the first place or if we have inflated the importance of our solution with our own assumptions.

To find the audaciously desirable, we need to:

- Observe and reflect – to look closely at how our target customers are living out their daily lives, the jobs they need to do and the problems they face. Then dive deeper to derive their pain points and humbly face up to any misalignment of our product to ease the pain, or double down on the alignments;
- Imagine – to find inspiration from other sources, other industries and see if new ways of doing things can work in the current setting; and
- Dream big and take calculated risks – if the problem isn't big enough, it probably isn't worth solving.

As Steve Jobs once said to John Sculley while trying to hire him from Pepsi, "Do you want to sell sugar water for the rest of your life or come with me and change the world?"

If we think we are selling a product (such as sugar water), then our worldview is naturally narrowed to the scope conferred by that product. But if we think that we are answering a higher calling (to "change the world"), then we can use a bit of imagination, mix it up with lots of data from our observations, sprinkle a little of our reflections on what may work in different pockets of society and maybe, just maybe, we can think of something that will really bring a smile to our customers' faces, and push them to tell others about it.

And before we know it, what started off as a small experiment may just become a movement, a wave.

Once You have Started a Wave, ride it FAST

Your first ADO got you the attention of your customers, probably made you famous in the market, established you as a domain expert and a thought leader, got you the revenue traction you needed to prove to yourself, your team and prospective investors that you are on to something big. If you stop there, then you may be making the biggest mistake of your life as a founder.

What is demanded next of founders who have had a successful run from their first ADO may be even more challenging than coming up with the ADO in the first place. This is because they then need to work really quickly to build on this success and offer the next ADO, almost with the intent to disrupt the current product. It's more than just adding features to the current product. Unless these features fundamentally adjust the way the product is used or better the current user experience phenomenally, they represent only incremental changes to the ADO and competitors will soon be doing the same and catching up.

For this reason, we find successful mobile device companies like Samsung and Apple offering new versions of their smartphones each year, with each iteration promising some new features that will wow their users: sharper images like never before, some crazy filters that produce amazing image and video effects, an enlarged ecosystem to widen the use case, some bundled-in features that make the devices perform actions that could not be done in the past. The list goes on.

But even industry legends may not get it right every time.

We know Apple as probably the world's most successful computer company but not every product that Steve Jobs envisioned and launched has been successful. For example, Apple launched iBooks in 2010 to disrupt the e-book space. The product was impressive and the interactivity potential of each iBook was unmatched in its time. To readers, iBooks looked like a gamechanger and could easily qualify as an ADO. But ten years after its launch and lots of marketing dollars spent, Apple decided to shut it down. I will discuss why iBooks failed while iTunes was a huge success in Chapter 4 "The Story of a Business".

There is a saying in Chinese: 创业难、守业更难 – translated: "It's tough to start a business, but it's even tougher to guard it." Before our ADO, no one could see how awesome an experience it could bring to the lives of our customers. Once the market has witnessed what our ADO can do, competitors will rush in and before we know it, competitors ranging from established companies to new startups will be attempting to take a piece of what we have created. What was once a blue ocean that we have discovered can quickly turn into a red ocean in a matter of a few years, or even a few months.

So how can we stay ahead of the pack when our market has become crowded with competitors? I will explore that in the next chapter.

3

From Red to Blue

How to Position a Venture in a Crowded Space

In their analysis of market dynamics, the authors of *Blue Ocean Strategy*,[19] W Chan Kim and Renée Mauborgne, described any given market as between a blue ocean and a red ocean. A blue ocean is a market or industry that is untapped or unexplored or possibly not in existence, with high potential for growth. One example of a company that has successfully implemented a blue ocean strategy is Cirque du Soleil. Rather than competing in the crowded and mature circus industry, Cirque du Soleil created a new market by blending elements of traditional circus acts with theatre, dance and live music to create a unique, high-end performance experience. This allowed the company to charge premium prices for tickets and generate significant revenue.

On the other hand, a company in a red ocean is one that is competing in a crowded and well-established market, making it difficult to differentiate itself and capture market share. An example of this is a traditional bricks and mortar retail store, which faces intense competition from both online and offline retailers. These companies are often forced to compete on price, which can lead to

---

19   W Chan Kim & Renée Mauborgne, *Blue Ocean Strategy – How to Create Uncontested Market Space and Make the Competition Irrelevant* (Harvard Business Review Press, 2005).

thin margins and make it difficult to stand out from the competition. Another example would be the telecommunications industry, where a large number of players are present and they are fighting for the same customers by providing similar products and services. There is intense competition to gain and retain customers, leading to pricing wars and heavy marketing expenses.

As mentioned in the previous chapter, despite having a great run with an ADO, a company can quickly be caught up by its competitors if it isn't fast enough to offer the next ADO to stay ahead of the competition. A once blue ocean can quickly turn into red.

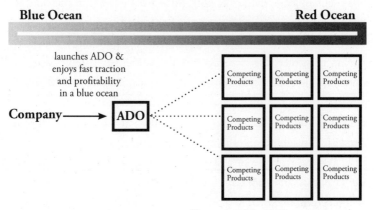

The success of the ADO attracts competitors, that quickly enter the market with products that compete for market share. Despite being of lower quality and brand value, the market soon becomes a crowded red ocean.

Yet, with innovative thinking and a bit of imagination, businesses can find blue oceans. This chapter explores the paradigms that a new venture founder should have when starting a venture in a space that is crowded with competitors.

Let's begin our discussion on the question of competition. Who are we competing against? And do we see our business as a niche one when it may be competing in a mass market?

Know Who You are Up Against – Determining Niche from Mass

Some entrepreneurs whom I have spoken with have the impression that a niche opportunity is a small one and one where they are likely to chance upon a blue ocean, while a mass opportunity is often a crowded red ocean.

To make sense of this, we may need to think about how we evaluate a niche market and whether a niche business is really that "niche" after all.

Just how do we look at a business opportunity to determine if it is a niche or mass market opportunity? To answer this question, we need to look at our business from a functional standpoint by asking ourselves: what function does this (service or product) serve to the paying customer? Or, as Clayton Christensen suggested:[20] what *job* does the customer get done with this service we provide? When we evaluate through a functional lens, we may start to see just who we are competing against in that target market, and it may unveil some surprising insights along the way.

Take the example of a startup that I spoke to some time back. Let's call this company EduLunar, whose primary market is the public schools sector in North Asia. The company is led by a visionary founder who has managed to use some pretty cool tech to help teachers build and manage learning material online for students. EduLunar's tech allows teachers to easily upload test questions by simply writing on paper and scanning the handwritten questions with the app. The app's AI engine would intelligently turn these questions into digital form for management by the teacher, who can distribute them to her students as homework and assignments via the app. The app also boasts a rich collection of thousands of questions in a massive bank that is placed at the teacher's disposal. EduLunar's founder thought of her company as a tech company in a niche market, possibly because she hadn't found others who used tech in this way in the education scene and so there didn't seem to be many competitors in this space.

20   Clayton M Christensen, Taddy Hall, Karen Dillon & David S Duncan, *Competing Against Luck – The Story of Innovation and Customer Choice* (Harper Business, 2016).

I thought otherwise.

I asked about who she thought her competitors were and what business she was in. Simply: was EduLunar in the tech business or the content business? And was it competing with other tech companies or content publishers?

Initially, the answer seemed obvious: an education technology company that competed with other edtech companies to meet a very specific need of teachers. This made it a tech business for education, which seemed pretty niche. But a closer look through the lens of what job(s) the users were trying to get done with EduLunar revealed that the users were using EduLunar's tech to create, distribute and manage content for their students.

Yes, content.

And the tech was only a means to make that happen. Another way of looking at it could be that EduLunar's users were not head over heels on the tech as much as the content they could get their hands on to get their job done.

If content was the point of using EduLunar, then we needed to ask just which content companies EduLunar had to fight against to get the users' attention and to get users paying for its service. The list of competitors wasn't short: basically, any content creator, publisher (print or otherwise) would be competing for the same users' attention and wallet.

So what first appeared to be a niche opportunity had turned out to be a pretty mass opportunity, since the same teacher that found EduLunar's content repertoire useful might have found those offered by other publishers just as useful. And the prices that those publishers charged could have been very low.

This looked very much like a red ocean (well, at least an orange one) to me and I suspected she could have faced a hard time bringing in revenue from a large number of users, given the choices these users might have had with other players offering to get the same job done.

Just Who are We Competing with?

I was in contact with a company in the food and beverage industry that started a meal-as-a-service or meal delivery service during the COVID-19 pandemic. Let's call this company HomeChef.

Customers of HomeChef would subscribe to a plan and decide on the number of meals to be delivered weekly in one batch to a specified location. They only need to heat each meal in a microwave oven for four minutes and it would be ready to eat. Each meal can last for one week in the refrigerator and each week, subscribers will choose which dishes they would like delivered. The menu changes every week and each meal is of a restaurant grade. The price isn't cheap at $12 per meal but the product is great and I am a fan who likes it enough to tell my friends about it.

Sales, however, have been flat.

I met with the management, who explained that they were competing with other healthy food delivery providers. Both HomeChef and their competitors target health-conscious gym goers, and their competitors weren't doing well either. They reckoned that it was because of the small market (healthy gym goers) that appreciated this service at that price point.

I saw it differently.

From what I could see, HomeChef's product solved a big problem for me: prior to subscribing to this service, I needed to get on to a food delivery app every day to order a meal for delivery to either my office or my home (on days when I worked from home). This happened every day and the cost would amount to almost $20 per meal with delivery charges included. Even worse, it was hard to find a meal that was tasty and healthy, so I ended up mostly eating the same few dishes by alternating between them. This service solved all that for me. It didn't require me to make difficult choices each day and I felt satisfied with a restaurant-grade cooked meal that was friendly on the waist which, at my age, is a tough problem to crack!

So how can this service be competing only with companies that offer delivery of healthy meals to gym-going or yoga-attending customers who are keen to lose weight? It should be competing against the food delivery apps that the general office worker uses to order in lunch, and that market is huge. Plus, considering that the price point seems competitive, this company could potentially disrupt this space by giving their customers a choice that is friendlier on the wallet (and waist). HomeChef could carve a blue ocean within a red one, as did Cirque du Soleil.

With HomeChef and EduLunar, we can see that by reframing the business according to the problem it is trying to solve and the job to be done by the customer, the competition landscape can look very different. In EduLunar, the founders eventually realised that they were competing in a red ocean when they initially thought they had a niche advantage, while in HomeChef, the founders didn't notice a blue ocean forming in a crowded market.

Sometimes, reframing our competition can help to open new opportunities that can help us discover a blue ocean or even disrupt those in the red ocean, simply because we are a new entrant to the scene with no prior baggage.

Getting to a Blue Ocean in a Crowded Space

There is no straightforward answer to this question of how to get to a blue ocean in a crowded space, but one way I have found to work quite well has been to delve deep and think laterally to qualify interesting opportunities that can be served by the core technology, machinery or competencies behind the products and services we offer to our customers.

In the book *Competing for the Future*,[21] authors Gary Hamel and CK Prahalad advocated analysing a business in terms of the functional units or core competencies of the company instead of its product lines. Once the core competencies are known, the management would be able to evaluate just what the company can do to deploy them to serve

---

21   Gary Hamel & CK Prahalad, *Competing for the Future* (Harvard Business School Press, 1994).

new markets, find new opportunities within the current markets, get the job done for new and potential customers in the same space but in a way that others have not already done so at that time – finding the blue ocean in a seemingly red one.

Helping EduLunar Get from Red to Blue

Recall that EduLunar's customers were teachers who didn't mind spending money to benefit their students. We could argue that the teachers were the paying customers but not really the end user.

This is where the unit economics didn't quite add up: it would be very challenging to get enough teachers to buy the product and generate revenue for EduLunar that justifies a decent valuation to an investor or prospective buyer. This is because each teacher typically leads anywhere from 40 to 200 students. It means that the final end user number can be up to 200 times the actual paying customer number. The burden of servicing 200 users per one paying customer may not add up, unless the company is highly efficient in the way it manages data and is able to charge a higher fee to the paying teacher, who may already be paying out of her own pocket. Given that EduLunar's primary market is the public schools sector in North Asia, the customer's wages may not be able to sustain a higher subscription fee on the product.

But the company has a great piece of AI-driven tech that could make the entire way of managing homework outside of the classroom work perfectly for students. With a little more development, EduLunar could fashion the tech to automark and grade handwritten answers that are submitted by students. No expert help from the teacher would be needed, which means that just about anyone can manage this learning process for their child at home.

Thus, instead of targeting the teachers, EduLunar could target enthusiastic parents in Asia who are keen to know how their children are faring after school hours, and to help these parents do so in a super-fast and highly productive way. Allowing parents to access the massive question bank with just one subscription also makes the product audaciously desirable. Once the focus is shifted to parents, the unit economics would work quite differently and could potentially open new opportunities for the company.

Same piece of tech – a different target customer in the same space of after-school lessons.

EduLunar's Core Competencies

AI-powered	Rich Question Bank
Grading engine	AI Domain expertise

Helping HomeChef See Blue in Red

Then let's look at the meal-as-a-service business of HomeChef. The core competencies can be seen in the exhibit below. In addition to a solid product, the company has two key assets in its favour:

ASSET 1. A flourishing multimillion-dollar catering business that serves corporations everywhere in the country. This is a powerful resource as each corporation is a host to many of such potential customers and already each is an account managed by the catering division. It drastically lowers the customer acquisition costs as compared to their competitors who lack such a channel. Its network of delivery drivers for its catering business also means it can potentially drastically reduce the delivery costs that can contribute up to 20 per cent of the operating costs. This will allow it to expend more resources to get into into new markets with even more competitive pricing and potentially disruptive business models. I will discuss how such assets are extremely valuable to a new venture in Chapter 5 "Make Your Numbers Talk" and Chapter 8 "Going to Market".

ASSET 2. A solid network of more than 20 restaurants throughout the country, offering different cuisines from Southeast Asian to

Japanese and international flavours. This provides the company with a powerful capability to offer a wide menu to its customers for its meal-as-a-service business, something that many of its competitors who are just starting out may not be able to keep up with.

HomeChef's Core Competencies

Huge central kitchen	Huge base of corporate customer	Expansive network of resturants across the country
Domain expertise across different meal types	Network of delivery drives	

With HomeChef, the challenge is to get to the right segment of the market and make the product known. Then to constantly engage with the customers to get a clear sense of what needs to be tweaked in order to attain an NPS of more than 8.5 consistently.

A lesson learned: how I failed to break through a red ocean

By now, you would have heard me talk about my life sciences education enrichment venture that I started in 2000 and how it grew tremendously because of our ADO that got schools rushing to sign on with us. But soon after, competitors started entering the market, claiming to offer similar services. Together, they were able to carve away some market share from us, although we remained the market leader in this space with some of the highest paying clients staying on with us, mainly because of the credibility and the product standard that became synonymous with our brand. But the market was soon looking like a red ocean.

Very early on, I had foreseen the impending competition and wanted to double down to develop another offering that was just as desirable. So, the company reinvested all its profits into research and development. We expanded our team and hired new people in other fields of expertise, such as digital content and tech development. We were especially steeped in investing in e-learning and digital animation, where we saw an opportunity for us to take life sciences learning to the mainstream media – on TV and online.

Unfortunately, I misread the situation. At that time, our team failed to nail down just what and whose jobs we were trying to get done. We had thought that by presenting the same type of content in highly engaging ways for children, we would get more sales and we would establish a moat around our offering, making it hard for others to emulate. But in hindsight, we were solving the problem for the wrong party. Our clients were, in fact, the schools and their teachers, who already felt inadequate to teach their students these complex concepts. That was why they had hired us. Having a nice cartoon animation to add to our repertoire of teaching resources would make the product better, but not transform the way it was being used in the classroom. It would not produce disproportionately better results that was expected of an ADO.

So, we didn't get it right, despite spending lots of money on R&D and acquiring one of our competitors. Soon after, we began losing market share to our competitors. We also tried to expand to other markets, in search of blue oceans there but that didn't work as well (more on this in Chapter 8 "Going to Market".)

This episode forced us to return to the drawing board and to look closely at our customers and the problems that they needed to deal with on a daily basis. Three years later, in our third venture within the same company, we finally saw the jobs that our target customers needed to get done and offered another ADO that got us a line of great contracts with ministries of education and governments in Asia and the Middle East.

Then five years after that, we offered another ADO in our fourth venture. This led to a nice licensing deal and an exit from an investment we made along the way, sustaining the company on a profitable course (read more about that in Chapter 10 "The Exit – Sell, Float or Close").

The point I am trying to make here is that iterating one ADO after another to break out of a crowded market (that ironically resulted from the success of the first ADO) is tough work. But that's the only way to stay ahead and the founder needs to motivate his or her team to be attentive, crazily customer-centric and to work at lightning speed.

Speed is really a strategic asset during these times if we are aiming for our enterprise to qualify for an exit in 36 months from founding.

Reframing of Value Proposition to Uncover New Opportunities

Sometimes, we need to think hard to find a specific problem to solve in a mass market, and when we are able to do so, we may unlock the gate to an opportunity that others have not yet noticed, because we can get the job done for our target customers. As entrepreneurs, the burden is on us to constantly be on the lookout for signs that suggest we may be barking up the wrong tree, and to be decisive to change course quickly. History is filled with endeavours of innovators who saw an opportunity amidst an apparent failure, from the discovery of antibiotics to the creation of the "blue pill" (Viagra).

To be clear, the process isn't straightforward and is often painful to the entrepreneur as it means re-evaluating the premise of his or her narrative and assumptions. In the midst of all the other operational demands, it can be a tough journey. Sometimes, having someone else from the outside provide advice can help, but it is important to choose the right person to join in the conversation.

In Chapter 6 "Bootstrapping – Beg, Borrow, Build, Deal", I will discuss some considerations for finding the right people to help founders start the new venture and bootstrap it to a point that could be attractive to investors to help take it further.

First, however, it is important to know what makes up a growth narrative of an enterprise and how these facets form the growth story of a new venture.

SECTION 2
THE PLAN

4

The Story of a Business
Facets of a Growth Narrative

To launch and exit in 36 months, the business of an enterprise must be designed for rapid and sustainable growth with the potential of an exit for its shareholders in the foreseeable future. This is not a simple process as the founders will need to dig deep and think through the entire business concept and model. Sometimes, we can get carried away thinking that we have a good piece of technology and that's all it takes to win.

Let's consider if this assumption is true.

We begin by looking at four companies which fought on three battlefronts.

Four Companies, Three Battlefronts
Battlefront #1:
In December 2009, Steve Jobs met with Dropbox founder, Drew Houston, and his partner, Arash Ferdowsi, at a meeting in Apple's Cupertino office. At that meeting, Jobs told them that Dropbox was only a feature and not a product.[22] Jobs offered to acquire Dropbox

---

22   Victoria Barret, "Dropbox: The Inside Story Of Tech's Hottest Startup" Forbes (18 October 2011) <https://www.forbes.com/sites/victoriabarret/2011/10/18/dropbox-the-inside-story-of-techs-hottest-startup/?sh=1d542e556437>.

and Houston rejected the offer. Jobs told Houston that if acquisition wasn't possible, Apple would go after Dropbox.[23] Before parting ways, Houston and Jobs agreed to meet again. That second meeting didn't take place. In June the following year, Steve Jobs revealed iCloud as the solution of choice over Dropbox to get all our files, from all our devices, into one place. Yet, DropBox went on to IPO in 2018 at a valuation of more than US$9 billion. So it looks like Dropbox survived Apple's attack on its core product.

Battlefront #2:

In the early 2000s, Creative Technology, a Singapore-based company, was a leading manufacturer of MP3 players and had developed its own proprietary technology for playing digital music files. Apple, on the other hand, was just starting to enter the MP3 player market with its iPod product line. In 2005, Creative sued Apple for patent infringement, alleging that Apple had used its technology in the iPod without permission. In 2007, Apple settled the matter with Creative for $100 million.[24] Creative's founder, Sim Wong Hoo felt that this settlement was a "consolation prize" and not a win.[25] He might have been right, as Apple continued to dominate the MP3 player market with its iPod products, then the iPhone, while Creative's market share declined. Creative eventually pivoted from the MP3 market.

Battlefront #3:

We have all used a thumb drive or USB flash drive at some point in our lives. This handy device was actually invented in 2000 and sold under the brand name "ThumbDrive" by a company called

23 Jim Edwards, "Here's The $8 Billion Ending To Steve Jobs' Failed Attempt To Kill Dropbox" *Business Insider* (20 November 2013) <https://www.businessinsider.com/steve-jobs-once-vowed-to-kill-dropbox-now-its-worth-2013-11#:~:text=He%20told%20him%20he%20returned,going%20to%20come%20after%20Dropbox>.

24 Tom Krazit, "Apple settles with Creative for $100 million" CNET (24 August 2006) <https://www.cnet.com/tech/tech-industry/apple-settles-with-creative-for-100-million-1/>.

25 Natalie Teo, "Once upon a time, S'pore tech company Creative went up against Apple & walked away with US$100 million" Babelfish, Mothership.sg (5 January 2023) <https://babelfish.mothership.sg/creative-vs-apple-rip/>.

Trek Technology, based in Singapore.[26] But Trek's ThumbDrive never gained the same level of popularity as the competing products. Today, Trek is hardly associated with the USB flash drive, which is still commonly used by people around the world as a convenient way to store and transfer digital files.

So, what did DropBox do differently that Creative or Trek might not have done? And what did Apple possess that made it almost invincible in its battles against Dropbox and Creative, despite looking like it had lost on both fronts?

"We have Great Design and Solid Tech" – So What?

It's not uncommon for companies to invent a new piece of cutting-edge technology or product, only to see it become more popular when it is adopted and marketed by other companies. Having superior tech may not, in itself, be sufficient for a company to dominate the market. In fact, in some cases, I would argue that tech is not the main play here, especially if the nature of the technology is software. These days, just about anyone with a budget of US$50,000 can develop very decent pieces of software – and $50,000 isn't a very high barrier to entry.

So, if tech isn't necessarily the make-or-break point in a company's growth, then what is?

To answer this question, we need to explore the dimensions that make up a compelling growth story of a scalable venture. In this chapter, I discuss five main dimensions of a growth story:

1. Having access to a thriving ecosystem;
2. The problem with friction;
3. Generating recurring revenue;
4. Framing the offering as an object-as-a-service; and
5. Operating in a network-based business model.

---

26   Hallam Stevens, "Who Really Invented the Thumb Drive?" IEEE Spectrum (10 December 2022) <https://spectrum.ieee.org/thumb-drive>.

Growth Story Dimension #1: Having Access to a Thriving Ecosystem

The concept of an ecosystem has its roots in nature, where living organisms depend on each other to survive. In a stable ecosystem, there are organisms that feed on other living organisms and there are those that are being fed on. The business world operates in very much the same way, and we can learn a lesson or two from how natural ecosystems work. There is one difference though: in nature, everyone wants to avoid being eaten or consumed, while in business, anyone who offers something in the market will wish to be consumed as soon as possible.

One way to represent an ecosystem is a food web. Let's look at a simple example below.

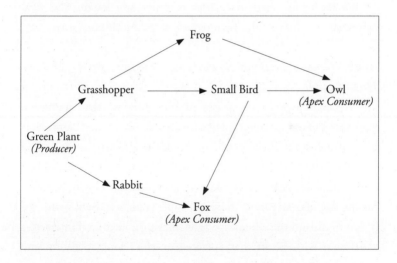

As you can see from the diagram above, except for the green plant and the apex consumer, all organisms need to feed on something and, in turn, will be fed on. Now, imagine each organism in the food web as a type of business. In a business ecosystem, this network may comprise suppliers, distributors, customers, competitors and other stakeholders that operate within a specific industry or market. A company that supplies to its customers upstream in the network may be a customer to another company downstream.

Companies that own and operate ecosystems are able to offer new products and services to their customers at relatively lower cost because they can access these customers. At the same time, they can command a premium from other suppliers that wish to tap on their ecosystems. Companies that do not own and operate such ecosystems will need to spend precious dollars in advertising on these platforms and sharing substantial revenue with them on each sale. All these add to the cost of acquiring a customer or the Customer Acquisition Cost (CAC). The lesser the access to the target customer in the ecosystem, the higher the CAC. So, the goal is to access the target customers at the lowest cost and the quickest way possible.

But having the ecosystem alone may not be enough. And what better way to illustrate this than to look at the Apple ecosystem.

Apple iTunes and iBooks Shared the Same Ecosystem – Only One Made It

The Apple ecosystem comprises its operating systems, hardware, App Store, iTunes store, Apple Music, Apple Arcade and, some time back, iBookstore. The iTunes store took the industry by storm and disrupted the song recording industry. Today, iTunes remains one of the most successful music marketplaces, despite being only meant for the Apple device user. In 2010, Apple launched iBooks with the intent to disrupt the e-book space by offering a next-level interactive experience with books that operated on the iBooks platform and accessed from the iPad. From a user perspective, the experience was really quite awesome with the user able to read the text while interacting with videos and other animated presentations on the same page. But this offering didn't gain traction and ten years later, the iBooks app and iBooks store were officially shut down. So what does iTunes have over iBooks that allowed it to be so successful?

Content. Lots of it.

The stumbling block with iBooks was the need for content to be redesigned into the iBooks format. Although iBooks had a great structure of presenting book content that was amazingly interactive and multi-dimensional for its time, the requirement for a redevelopment of the content before it could be offered to the target customer drastically slowed the process of adding new content to the ecosystem, not to mention the astronomical costs associated with the process. Publishers were not keen to invest heavily in an opportunity to sell to a subset of customers who used Apple products.

Using the matrix of analysing competition from the perspective of "jobs to be done" for the customer, we can see that iBooks faced a conundrum of having customers on both sides: suppliers (the publishers) and readers. Both sets of customers have different jobs that need done and iBooks wasn't able to enable the publishers to quickly and efficiently get their content into a hyper-interactive format as it was promised to readers.

We are seeing a similar pattern with AppleTV, where subscribers can watch AppleTV productions but often need to pay a premium to watch other third-party content. It makes the content repertoire limited at the outset and as the volume of release of new shows is not comparable to that of competitors like Netflix and Amazon, AppleTV will find it hard to keep up with the competition.

A Huge User Base Does Not Make a Solid Ecosystem

Some years back, when I was running a venture that produced interactive books for children, we collaborated with a telco that had a significant market share in the country. We figured that with their large subscriber base, coupled with their keen interest to build a marketplace for e-books, our interactive books would sell well.

We were wrong.

Despite marketing campaigns by the telco, sales were dismal to say the least, and it baffled us and their marketing team.

This same telco had another service that allowed its customers to purchase movies on demand, to be played on the TV. The process of purchase was simple and almost immediate – the customer browsed through the catalogue on the TV, then selected the movie to watch, confirmed the purchase (which would be reflected in the bill at the end of the month), and watched it immediately on the TV. This offer didn't need much marketing and did very well for the telco.

At the same time, a competing telco also launched its own e-book store, relying on their equally large customer base. Both telcos had to shut their e-book stores down after two years of failed attempts.

So what went wrong with the e-book business in these telcos? And why do members of the same ecosystem respond so differently to the offers by the same operator?

The culprit: friction.

Growth Story Dimension #2: Friction

Many entrepreneurs fall into the trap of thinking that when they have access to a large customer base, they can sell anything to that base and expect good sales. They fail to consider an important element in the adoption process: friction.

Friction, in this case, refers to the hurdles or inertia experienced by the customer in using the product or service provided by the supplier. The higher the friction in adoption, the greater the energy required of the customer.

The more the company does for the customer, the lesser friction for the customer and the greater the likelihood the customer will adopt the service. Conversely, the more the customer has to work independently without assistance from the company, the greater the inertia and the lower the price needed to get a customer to adopt it.

In the telco's e-book store, the customers needed to procure their own device and set it up before they could download the bought item to read. Compare this with the movie on-demand offering that can be accessed almost immediately after selection, on the same device used to watch other movies. It is clear to see which offering is more likely to get adoption quicker and cheaper.

These days, many businesses want to be a platform or marketplace of sorts. Many entrepreneurs seem to think that by merely setting up the infrastructure for such a marketplace, the platform will somehow thrive on its own. Even companies with a large, ready pool of subscribers seem to think that it is easy to launch their marketplace to the subscriber base and expect traction from day one. But we know from experience that this is rarely the case.

For a marketplace to work, getting hold of the products offered must be as frictionless as possible. Simply having the infrastructure for the marketplace, having access to a large pool of potential customers and even having a powerful marketing engine will not be enough if it takes too much effort on the part of the customer to access the products in that marketplace. The entire shopping-to-buying-to-using experience is an integral part that makes a product or service audaciously desirable.

Attributes of a successful ecosystem	
Supply Side	Demand Side
Frictionless onboarding by suppliers.	Rich and diverse product repertoire.
Access to a huge customer base.	Frictionless access-to-use experience by the customer.

Growth Story Dimension #3: Value of Recurring Revenue

When a customer buys from us again, it's a good sign as it suggests that whatever we are offering is valuable enough for them to return to buy more. But when a customer commits to paying us on a regular basis, it suggests that the same customer could remain with us for a much longer period and thus the value of this person across his or her "lifetime" as our customer increases disproportionately. This increase in the Lifetime Value (LTV) of the customer consequently increases the perceived value of the business. It can happen because our business is collecting recurring revenue.

Recurring revenue is an income stream where customers commit to pay for a product or service on a regular basis, such as on a monthly or annual basis, hence the name "recurring".

The longer the period of recurring revenue, the higher the perceived value of the business. Thus, recurring revenues that we collect each year (annual recurring revenue or ARR) is much more valuable than monthly recurring revenue (MRR). MRR, in turn, is more valuable than repeat one-time purchases.

Perceived value of different types of revenue						
Annual recurring revenue	>	Monthly recurring revenue	>	Repeated one-time purchases	>	One-time unrepeated purchase

Recurring revenues also have an operational role in the company as they enable the company's management to predict cash flows and plan with a greater peace of mind that money will not run out unexpectedly. Because of this property, recurring revenue is a strong indicator of a company's ability to generate consistent, predictable revenue over time and is often considered to be a key metric of viability and growth of the company.

Recurring revenue often takes the form of subscription or service fees that are paid either upfront or billed periodically (such as weekly, monthly, quarterly or yearly). As far as possible, we should try to structure our business to make recurring revenue over one-off service revenue.

Growth Story Dimension #4: Frame Offering as Object-as-a-Service

When we sell a product, say from a store, the customer pays us just once, until he or she returns to buy from us again. The same applies to a service (like at the car wash or in a restaurant). If that customer does not return to buy from us again, we lose any prospect of making any more money off her. Because of this risk and the lack of clarity whether we can ever get a consistent flow of revenue from the same customer, an enterprise that is in the business of selling items this way needs to sell a lot to prove that it has a value that is perceived to be attractive enough for investors who are looking to grow their investment by several folds in the future. So we see terms like Gross Merchandise Value (GMV) being used as a gauge for a company's value, based on the amount of sales it can generate from customers on a one-time basis. These companies need to generate a lot of GMV, often in the hundreds of millions or even billions of dollars before they can be considered valuable enough.

A more viable way to design a scalable business is through an offering that generates revenue on a recurring basis, and one way to do this is to design the product as a service. Offering a product-as-a-service works a bit like offering a product out for hire, where the hirer pays the provider a fixed fee to use the product for a limited period of time, and the provider provides all the services to ensure that the product works as it promises.

Almost anything can be framed as a service, as long as customers are willing to forgo owning it and paying a lower fixed fee over a period of time to enjoy all the peripheral services while getting to use the product for its intended purpose. Even consumables like food, razor blades and even toothbrushes have been successfully offered as subscription-based services:

1. Freshly is a meal-as-a-service company that provides fully cooked, healthy meals delivered directly to customers which can be reheated in a few minutes. It was acquired by Nestle in 2020 in a deal worth up to $1.5 billion.[27]
2. Dollar Shave Club is a men's razor blade subscription service that allows customers to receive regular shipments of high-quality razors and other grooming products at a fraction of the cost of traditional brands. The company was acquired by Unilever in 2016 for a reported $1 billion,[28] which was about five times its forecasted revenue for that year.
3. Quip, Goby and Gloridea, companies operating in the US and Asia, offer some of the more popular electric toothbrush subscription services with replacement brush heads delivered every two months to subscribers.

Growth Story Dimension #5: Power of a Network-Based Business

In a network-based business, a company derives its revenue and ultimately its value from its network of customers, users or partners. In this type of business, the more users or customers that join the network, the more valuable the network becomes, as it creates network effects. These network effects can take several forms, such as the ability to connect more people, the ability to share information more easily or the ability to create more valuable services and products. Network-based businesses can also generate revenue through various ways, such as by charging transaction fees, advertising, licensing its technology or data, and/or providing value added services to its customers/users, making it a highly profitable business model.

As the size of a network increases, the value of the network increases at an even faster rate. For example, a social networking site

27   Anthony Ha, "Nestlé acquires healthy meal startup Freshly for up to $1.5B" TechCrunch+ (31 October 2020) <https://techcrunch.com/2020/10/30/nestle-acquires-freshly/>.
28   John Murray Brown & Arash Massoudi, "Unilever buys Dollar Shave Club for $1bn" *Financial Times* (20 July 2016) <https://www.ft.com/content/bd07237e-4e45-11e6-8172-e39ecd3b86fc>.

with ten users is much less valuable than one with ten million users. This phenomenon is known as increasing returns to scale. Because of this, network-based businesses have the potential to grow rapidly and become extremely valuable.

Another reason that network-based businesses can be valuable is because they can be difficult to replicate. A network's value comes from its users, so it can be hard for a new entrant to create a network with the same number of users or the same level of engagement. This can make it challenging for competitors to enter the market and create a viable alternative to an existing network-based business.

However, creating and scaling a network-based business is not an easy task as it requires lots of effort to build an ecosystem and to ensure that friction is reduced to the point where users find the product or service sticky enough to stay around and tell others about it. Entrepreneurs and new venture founders need to focus their attention on indicators that suggest if the product or the business model needs further tweaking to get to the point of increasing returns to scale.

Think lateral and find a gem in the backyard – the antique dealer

AntiquePlus is an antique dealing and appraisal business. Founded more than 30 years ago, it has since built a solid reputation in the region, providing antique appraisal and dealership services as well as running a small antique museum. The founder and his second-generation owners also conduct courses for hobbyists and professionals on the ways to evaluate different types of antiques. Revenue for the business has been flat over the years and the second-generation owners wanted to expand the revenue stream by providing more services, such as children's enrichment programmes to educate the next generation. So they approached me to help, but I didn't think that the education extension would contribute significantly to AntiquePlus's growth intent.

There was, however, something uniquely attractive about the company's assets that could help it develop a scalable business from a bricks-and-mortar base that they now possess – the company has, over the years, accumulated a database of more than 3,000 members. These members come from different backgrounds but they all have one thing in common: they are deeply interested in evaluating, collecting and selling antiques, and they need a platform to do all this conveniently.

So here is an opportunity for the company to develop a brand-new business: AntiquePlus could frame its business as a platform for the secondary antique market, where members pay a subscription fee to join a network of fellow collectors, and to trade their antiques on a regular basis. The company's appraisal service would double up to authenticate each artefact and validate the transaction.

While this platform isn't an online one like many other platforms, it qualifies as a network-based business. The more members it has, the more likely members will trade antiques within the network and the more ancillary services, such as antique appraisals, will be provided. Because of this, the value of the network increases.

Breaking Down the Three Battlefronts

Let's try to make sense of the battles between Dropbox/Creative against Apple, and Trek against the world.

Creative Technology, while having a solid piece of technology for MP3 players and navigation interface, lacked an ecosystem that allowed it to provide a seamless and integrated experience for its users. Apple's MP3 ecosystem for the iPod, on the other hand, spanned hardware, software, services, music companies and other content providers to provide users with a wide range of music and content. This helped to differentiate the iPod (and later, the iPhone and iPad) from other MP3 players and made it a more compelling choice for many consumers.

What about DropBox?

DropBox's marque product would have been just a feature as Steve Jobs had stated if it could only serve one of the operating systems amongst all others in the computing world. For example, if Dropbox was only good for the Apple operating system or the Android system, it would have been a feature for Apple or Android respectively. But that was not the case. Dropbox could cross different operating systems, allowing a user to open a file from any device, regardless of its operating system, and sync everything on the cloud. It became a cloud that would sync with the customer's "clouds". That is possibly why Dropbox could stand tall against the challenge of Apple's iCloud.

It can be argued that Steve Jobs might have been mistaken about the business of Dropbox. Dropbox was not in the business of cloud storage, a feature that was nested within the operating system of a family of devices. It was in the business of cloud syncing, a product that wasn't dependent on the clients' operating systems, but instead became the ecosystem within which these operating systems could reside and allowed content saved in Dropbox to be interoperable. It didn't need elaborate distribution channels as long as the users of other cloud-based services had a need to use them across different platforms. Dropbox was an ecosystem with low friction for adoption and, in being so, it became a sticky product. Its business model of offering cloud storage-as-a-service also enables it to charge recurring fees to its users.

Yet, it is not alone in this space. Far from it. Dropbox now needs to compete with Microsoft and Google for customers and it is increasingly difficult to out-manoeuvre them. So it needs to have more services to make it more sticky in this space, where things happen so fast. While it remains to be seen how Dropbox will fare in the years to come, it has certainly been able to grow despite Steve Jobs' subtle warning back in 2009.

In the case of Trek's thumb drive, Trek Technology was a small company and did not have the resources to market and distribute the ThumbDrive on a large scale. As a result, the product did not gain widespread adoption and remained relatively unknown to most consumers. This gave other companies in Europe, US and China, which saw the potential of the thumb drive, the opportunity to make their own versions of the product. These companies had more resources and were able to effectively promote and sell their thumb drives, which helped to drive widespread adoption of the technology. While Trek might have patents protecting its invention, enforcing these patents against its competitors would have been too costly for them to pursue.

A great growth narrative goes beyond having a solid product, or even a great piece of technology that can be protected by patents, as can be seen in the cases of Creative Technology and its MP3 player and Trek Technology and its thumb drive.

A solid business that is poised for growth is often powered by an ADO that extends beyond a singular product or service to include an entire ecosystem of players, all working seamlessly together to offer a total and riveting experience for the customer, who is happy to pay for the service over and over again. This generates recurring revenue that is very valuable to the enterprise.

Framing a Growth Narrative

To frame a growth narrative for our enterprise, we need to ask ourselves:

- What does our enterprise or its founders possess that allow us to access a large pool of potential users?
- Do we intend to operate an ecosystem? If so, what do we have on hand that can enable us to onboard lots of choices for our target customers prior to the launch of our product? How long will it take for us to reach that state?
- How easy is it for our target users to use the service we provide? Is it a "done for them", a "done with them" or a "do it themselves" service?
- Is it a one-time sale or a recurring service?
- Do we operate a network-based system, where our pool of customers increases with an increase in the pool of suppliers in our network? If not, then is there something in our business that may enable us to operate a network-based business?
- Are we a supplier within an established network? If so, how can we continue to access more customers within that network over time?

As almost every venture deals with money, a sound growth narrative needs to be corroborated by financial indicators. You will find that numbers do tell a story about an enterprise, as we shall explore in the next chapter.

5

Make Your Numbers Talk

A Dollar a T-shirt – One Billion Dollars from China

On my way home from the airport one day, after a trip to Beijing on business, the cab driver shared with me that he had always wanted to sell T-shirts in China. I suspected that he wanted to tell me this after finding out that I had returned from China on a business trip. He reasoned that with more than 1 billion people in China, even if one person would pay him $1 for a T-shirt, he would be a billionaire.

He wasn't wrong, numerically at least.

Where he might be mistaken is that on the same street where he sells his T-shirts, there are probably at least a dozen or more folks selling the same thing, at lower prices, in a wider variety of colours. So how does he plan to beat them and still make that $1 billion that he had originally anticipated?

"Oh, I didn't think of that," the excitement in his voice faded and there was silence for the rest of the journey.

In this exchange, our friendly cab driver understood what I have learned over two decades as a serial venture founder, that just because a market is huge doesn't mean it is yours to take.

When we have a misconstrued idea of the market and are uninformed about the profitability of our business, the venture will inevitably run itself to the ground. If we are lucky, this would happen soon after we start, before we take on other people's money and without causing us to lose a lot of our own money. But if the process drags on and we take on other people's money, provide personal guarantees to loans without knowing which financial metrics to pay attention to in order to turn our venture around, the eventual outcome could be very painful.

In this chapter, we explore four of the most important financial metrics that paint a picture of our enterprise's potential for growth and how they can help us design a venture that scales nicely while making money, or to help us analyse a distressed venture to turn it around.

For readers not trained in corporate finance, this is a chapter written by a layman for the layman. So for accountants and those who are trained in corporate finance, you may skip this chapter.

How Real is the Opportunity?
TAM, SAM, SOM

Anyone who has raised funds or has been guided by startup accelerators will be familiar with TAM, SAM and SOM as terms we commonly use to size up the market that we target. This kind of analysis is especially useful when talking to investors who have little to no knowledge of our business and need to see if the target markets are interesting enough for them to consider investing.

Total Addressable Market (TAM) refers to the total demand for a product or service within a particular market. This includes all potential customers who could benefit from using the product or service anywhere in the world. It doesn't matter whether these customers are using a competing product or if you can even reach them. TAM is also known as the total available market.

Serviceable Addressable Market (SAM) refers to the portion of the total available market that a company expects to serve. As SAM takes into account the ability of the company to reach and serve the customers in a target market, this value is smaller than TAM. Typically, SAM can be derived from adding the sum of all potential customers for the offering and the average revenue that the providers can derive from them. SAM can give a more realistic estimate of the potential market size that the company can serve, as opposed to simply looking at TAM.

Servicable Obtainable Market (SOM) is a subset of SAM, representing a portion of the serviceable available market that a company can actually capture with its products or services. If the enterprise is already in business and is capturing some market share, then SOM can be derived from multiplying its share of the market by the SAM to give a sense of the potential market that the company can realistically capture, given its current position in the market. Of course, if the company is on track for rapid and exponential growth, then this way of calculating may underestimate the SOM for the company, but it is a way to present a concrete picture of what the opportunity realistically looks like for the company.

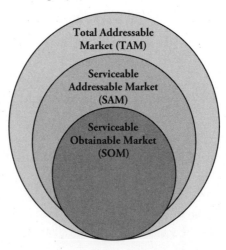

TAM, SAM and SOM are expressed in monetary terms, typically in the hundreds of millions or billions of dollars.

Deriving TAM

There are three main ways to derive the TAM for a business:

- By referencing data from third party research houses, such as IDC and Gartner, which conduct in depth research on the size and growth potential of different segments in different industries within a market. This may be considered by some fund managers as a somewhat lazy way to size a market. More on this in the later section of this chapter.
- For markets that are not mature, we can use the top-down approach, which starts by estimating the overall size of the market and then breaking it down into smaller segments to estimate the size of each segment now and in the future, based on its growth rate, before adding back these segments to derive the TAM.
- If we have a clear understanding of our target customers and their needs, we can adopt the bottom-up approach, which estimates the number of potential customers in each market segment and the amount they are prepared to pay for our product to derive a monetary value of that market segment as the number of customers multiplied by the anticipated amount each will spend on our product, before adding up the value of all relevant market segments.

Having access to a huge addressable market matters. A lot.

The China Government's crackdown on the private tutoring industry in July 2021 wiped out billions of value in China's education technology or edtech companies,[29] with several more billions stuck in China tutoring companies that have raised money from investors, mostly institutional ones over the past three years. One would have

---

29   Elliott Zaagman, "The casualties of China's education crackdown" TechCrunch+ (23 September 2021) <https://tcrn.ch/3kwwrXh>.

thought that many investors would panic and have even mulled over the possibility of ever investing in anything in China. "Not quite", according to my friend who's pretty senior in the investment community.

"Do you know how much money is sitting around for private equity investors to deploy in companies? I really don't think tens of billions of losses in this instance will kill anyone," he stated as a matter of fact.

"Furthermore, in these kinds of big-dollar investments, it is self-fulfilling", my friend continued, "and how it works is that these investors will keep putting in (money) to these companies until they succeed. And, of course, with a loaded war chest, these companies will go all out to burn and acquire customers and with each new peak in acquisition, the value of the company is elevated. All this is repeated over and over, until eventually the company exits by listing in the stock market, and until this end, they may still have not made any real money. So, let's imagine that you are that company and your current investors have a limitless bank account to support you through thick and thin. I am sure you too can succeed big time, right?"

These kinds of stories only take place in markets that are huge. Very huge. Like China or the US. The sheer size of the Chinese market, despite the unpredictability of policies, will not daunt daredevil investors from continuing to approach it.

If our addressable market is very small, investors are unlikely to place a high value on our enterprise, given our limited reach and "traction" (you will hear this word rattled out of investors' mouths all the time – it loosely translates to "how much you can get in a short period of time", and the measure of "how much" can be anything from users to subscribers to revenue, or anything that can suggest you can make money out of it).

So, if our business is good for only a small market, selling to only a small number of people, then its potential for growth is very limited. Consequently, its perceived value wouldn't be high, and therefore, it wouldn't be attractive to investors.

TAMs of Less than $1B may Make a Company Less Investable by Larger, Later-Stage Funds

Sebastian Duesterhoeft is a partner of Lightspeed Ventures, and whom some call the "Michael Jordan of TAM". In an interview by Mostly metrics[30], Duesterhoeft suggested that in a software-as-a-service (SaaS) business, "a $2.5B TAM opportunity is required to give an investor with a $500M fund the opportunity to have a 'fund-returner'", or a later-stage fund that is aiming to make an acceptable return on their investment. Extrapolating this after considering the possible market share gained by a leading SaaS business, it implies that even in an incredible achievement of a $1 billion exit for a company, "the absolute return dollars are often too small to move the needle enough" for a large fund. So, for founders who want to build highly scalable and fast-growing companies that could interest such investors, they often need to find a problem that is so systemic that it could impact the lives of humans across creeds, cultures, geographies and practices, and across industries. They need to show that their offerings are designed to target a multibillion-dollar TAM.

This isn't easy for two reasons.

Firstly, they may not have designed their offering to impact the lives of so many different groups of people everywhere in the world. Not many offerings can deliver such systemic impact. Ignoring this reality and using a broad-based approach such as high-level research reports to estimate as big a TAM as humanly possible isn't going to cut it for investors.

Secondly, even if their offering may be able to appeal to a wide range of audiences and it may be tempting to present the opportunity as a multibillion-dollar TAM, the founders may lack the capabilities to iterate their offering and capture even a significant subset of this market, simply because there are too many variables to consider and it makes the company look distracted, trying to capture too many pockets of opportunities all at once.

---

30   CJ Gustafson, "A Total Addressable Market (TAM) Masterclass" Mostly metrics (28 March 2023) <https://www.mostlymetrics.com/p/a-total-addressable-market-masterclass>.

I once met with a company that provided advanced counselling services for students. The founders were actively raising funds for this venture that aimed to meet this need using technology. They showed me the deck which stated that the TAM was worth several billions of dollars. I didn't quite agree with how they had derived the TAM and told them that the figure looked inflated. "But this is what VCs looking for unicorn potential targets want to see in an investment deck," was their reasoning. They may not be wrong. Yet, I felt that having inadvertently presented an inflated TAM without much basis could backfire as institutional investors are eagle-eyed at spotting such attempts.

Back to the interview with Sebastian Duesterhoeft, who had this to say about companies that used research reports as the main reference for deriving TAM:

> A big red flag for me is when founders simply use TAM numbers from Gartner/IDC in their pitch decks. More often than not, founders don't even know really what is included/excluded from those numbers and how the research firms came up with the estimates. Just using Gartner/IDC numbers likely means that you don't have a good sense yet for who you are selling to and how you should be pricing your product.

Thus, it is still better to begin with a realistic view of the TAM which we are targeting with our offering and then explore if the same offering, with a few tweaks, could solve another big problem in another industry, another context, with another set of customers. So how do we get the TAM right? To answer that, let's explore how we can get the TAM wrong.

Getting TAM Wrong

It is generally recommended to calculate TAM before SOM. This is because TAM provides estimates of the total market demand and the potential opportunity for your business. Once you have a clear understanding of the TAM, you can then calculate the SOM. This also means that getting a wrong estimation of the TAM can lead to flawed calculations of the SAM and SOM, and may give the founders and investors a misguided sense of the real commercial opportunity for the product or service that they are offering to the market.

The conventional and generally acceptable way of estimating TAM tends to overestimate the opportunity, resulting in an inflated SAM and SOM. Here are two examples.

Example #1: The Top-Down Approach

Let's take a hypothetical example of a mechanic who services new Honda cars that are less than one year old and let's use the top-down approach to estimate the TAM. Take the year 2017, when Honda sold slightly more than five million cars worldwide[31] That's how I would derive the TAM for the mechanic. But if the mechanic follows the conventional method of calculating TAM and has used the total number of cars sold in a year, regardless of brand (which works out to be more than 86 million cars),[32] to suggest a TAM, the opportunity is so inflated that any further derivation of the SOM would seem unrealistic.

It is thus important to clearly define the target market that our product is designed to serve to get a better estimate of the TAM. It is crucial that we avoid the pitfalls that could inflate our TAM calculations.

Then there is the issue with a "vertical TAM" and a "horizontal TAM". We sometimes hear this from investors when looking at the opportunity for a given business. Here, the concepts of vertical and horizontal refer to whether an opportunity exists within a certain

31 Mathilde Carlier, "Worldwide number of automobiles sold by Honda Group from FY 2002 to FY 2022" Statista (20 May 2022) <https://www.statista.com/statistics/267276/worldwide-automobile-sales-of-honda/>.

32 IEA, "Global car sales by key markets, 2005-2020" IEA, Paris (last updated 26 October 2022) <https://www.iea.org/data-and-statistics/charts/global-car-sales-by-key-markets-2005-2020>.

industry, market and segment, or whether it spans across different industries. This is important because TAMs that span across various industries (horizontal TAMs) logically tend to be a lot bigger than TAMs that are confined to just one industry (vertical TAMs). And companies whose businesses operate these horizontal TAMs would naturally seem a lot more interesting, investment-wise at least. But companies that operate within "vertical TAMs" can also be viewed as specialists in those industries and that can command a certain premium as well.

And it doesn't end there. There is also the argument of whether one should focus a specific domain within an industry to estimate its TAM before going more granular to estimate the SAM and SOM. There is really no one fixed way to estimate the TAM in such instances and the founder will just need to be able to justify how he or she derived the TAM and be prepared to argue should the person on the other side of the table disagrees.

For me, I like to estimate TAMs according to the specific domain within an industry where the expertise and offerings of my enterprise can serve customers well, instead of assuming that my enterprise is able to serve all customers within that industry. So my view is:

If you are in the business of ...	Don't size the TAM as ...
Servicing a particular brand of cars.	The entire car servicing industry worldwide, regardless of brands.
Providing student counselling services online.	The entire edtech industry worldwide, regardless of domain or services.
Delivering chilled products across the country.	The entire goods delivery service across every country in the world.

While you can get into the peripheral businesses, such as servicing other brands of cars in due course, you are not doing that now in your current business, unless it is within your business growth plan to do so. It is, therefore, crucial that we are prudent in sizing the TAM to accurately paint the picture of the real opportunity for us to capture in this business. No point kidding ourselves if our products and services are not designed to serve or address the needs of a significant part of the TAM we estimate it to be. And no point making the investor feel overly excited about the opportunity, or feel mildly deceived by the estimate.

Example #2: The Bottom-Up Approach

I met with a company that provided an online-based service for checking students' performance in non-academic domains. The founders shared their bottom-up approach for deriving the TAM, SAM and SOM for their business, based on the prices they were planning to charge their target customers. The numbers looked pretty impressive.

But I had a problem with it. I felt that this method of calculating the market opportunity rests on the assumption that the target customers are willing to pay for the product or service at the prices set by the company in its financial projections. What if the target customers did not have the purchasing power or did not feel that the prices offered were justifiable? So unless the company is able to support its pricing model by some real sales and feedback from customers, the TAM value derived may not be accurate or credible.

The bottom-up approach is useful when we have tested the product and its price points with our target customers and have secured at least some sales to prove that they are able to accept the offered price points.

Modelling the Business

Whenever I am asked to mentor startup founders of a new venture, I would always request to see the financial projections of the venture that they plan to set up. To me, this is the most concrete representation of the business, on where it takes in money (revenue streams), how much it needs to make the money (direct costs), how much expenses is required to run the business and the profit it could make at the end of each period. The model will also show me what the founders think is the probable growth pattern of its customer numbers over, say five years, giving me a sense of the growth potential of the venture. When I get to dive deeper into the numbers and the assumptions they make to justify those growth patterns and projected financial figures, I will get a sense of whether their projections are realistic or not.

The financial model of a business is quite a big document with several elements represented on an Excel spreadsheet or Google Sheet that spans the projected company's financial performance over three to five years. I won't go into the details of how to construct such a model here. Instead, let's explore some of these elements, what they mean and how we can use them to analyse, design and set targets to steer our business towards high growth and scalability. Here, I will discuss three metrics that are especially useful for a new venture founder: revenue, gross profit margin and EBITDA margin.

But before that, we need to get the unit economics right.

Get the Unit Economics Right

If revenue is an indicator of how much money a company can get from a customer, then the unit economics are the drivers that the company uses to get that money. Unit economics is a set of indicators which we use to analyse the profitability of a business by looking at the financial performance of a single unit of a product or service. It includes the revenue associated with selling one unit and the costs associated with making and delivering on that unit. Some examples of unit economics include:

- Price (and revenue) per unit of product;
- Cost of goods sold (COGS) per unit of product;
- Gross margin per unit of product; and
- Cost of acquiring one paying customer (CAC).

While just looking at unit economics may not paint a complete picture of a business, getting the unit economics right is key when we want to assess the value and viability of a business. As shown below, a business whose nature is seemingly scalable with major market share can actually be a huge red flag to an investor who is assessing its value.

When having 80 per cent market share is a huge red flag

Not too long ago, a friend of mine sought my advice on a deal he was asked to invest in. The investee was a company specialising in providing interactive digital content on the cloud for students in schools. The company had been around for a number of years and had excellent user traction. In the past 12 months, it had managed to get more than 80 per cent of target schools in its home territory to pay for its product. That worked out to close to 200,000 students, which was a respectable number.

The unit economics of the business, however, told a different story: the company's revenue over the same period was significantly less than $5 million, suggesting that its unit price wasn't high. With these numbers, it suggested that the value of its primary market was small (less than $5 million for 80 per cent market share), and a savvy investor would have reasons to doubt any significant upswing in the company's revenue going forward.

To mitigate this, the company recently launched a premium version of its product charged at more than five times the school price per unit. But conversion from school users to the premium package has been dismal and the bulk of its revenue remained derived from school users. When we looked at the premium offering versus the school offering, we didn't see a strong enough incentive for a user to pay so much more for a service whose low-priced version has already served more than what was expected.

Based on the stellar market share in local schools, it is clear that the core product is a very desirable one. But the question is, "Desirable to who? The teacher or the student?"

Because the core product is sold in schools, the decision makers are almost always the teachers in charge or the school leaders, and their needs are quite different from that of a parent. The low price of the product adds to its desirability and makes it a no-brainer to adopt it for the students, sometimes having a school pay for it on behalf of its students. This means that many parents have the impression that their children are getting this product for free. So to ask them to pay much more or to pay anything more for a premium version that doesn't boast a radically different and audaciously desirable experience isn't going to cut it for the parents.

So, when designing the business model and the core product of a venture, it is important to get the unit economics right. Prioritising market share without a clear, convincing and tested road map to increase the Lifetime Value (LTV) of each paying customer can be a huge strategic error that is challenging to turn around.

Modelling Revenue Growth

We derive the revenue for a business by multiplying two components:

the number of purchases over a specific period
x price for each purchase.

The number of purchases can take many forms, for example, over one month:

If your business is about …	"Number of purchases" could mean	"Price for each purchase" could refer to
Selling subscription-based products	Number of subscribers for that month	Subscription fees
Equipment or car rental	Total number of rental contracts signed that month whose rental period occurs within the same month	Rental fees
One-time purchase of a service/product	Number of transactions done in that month	Price of item or service

To model how revenue is likely to grow over the course of a year or more, we need to:

1. Estimate the number of customers who are likely to buy the product or service each month for the next 12 months in the First Year;

2. Multiply each number with the price we intend to charge to derive the revenue for that month;

3. Repeat this process for the Second Year, representing monthly projected revenue; and

4. Continue to do this for at least three more years, with quarterly projections from the Third Year onwards.

A Financial Model is only as accurate as the numbers we put in. If these values do not have a basis, then whatever we calculate to be the revenue on a month-on-month basis will not be credible. It is thus crucial for a founder to provide clear and defensible assumptions for the pattern of revenue growth, guided by the following questions:

- What is the basis for pricing our products/services this way, at this level? Are there references to suggest that our target customers will be willing to pay for our offerings at this price?

- What are we doing at different points in time, for different groups of customers, that will likely help us bring in these customers to pay for our offerings?

- What sort of conversion metrics would suggest that our assumptions for funnelling customers to pay for our offerings are reasonable?

- Who are we partnering with to help us get to the customers who are willing to pay us?

"Revenue Solves all Problems"

These are the words of a very wise and seasoned investor who invested in one of my earlier ventures. And he is right. In my experience, any venture that seeks a third party (not friends or family members) to support it financially will need to demonstrate at least one of the following by the time it goes to the market to look for funds:

- **Revenue**, which suggests that the service/product has a tangible value that people would pay for and has paid for it. This is the best indication to an investor in the early stages of a venture since any business idea remains no more than a thought and any vision remains no more than an image until someone actually pays for it to make it real and believable. However, if revenue is not possible at this stage (at the pre-revenue stage of the venture), you can consider the next option.
- **Proof of Revenue**, which is a pipeline of projects, customers or buyers for the product or service that will be delivered in due time. It is also called an order book and it should be supported by some form of documentation (a signed agreement or a pre-sale order is best) that lends credibility to the financial model and supports the asking valuation when you are looking to raise funds or exit the business.

Having revenue in the starting phases of a new venture beats not having any, unless the opportunity at hand is so obvious and big that investors are prepared to put money into a dream that hasn't been tested. Even so, having the right mix of business activities that generate good cash flow in the immediate term and those that bank on the future by building something that can disrupt the market will be important to help the company scale nicely.

But how can we get revenue when our product isn't completed in the first place?

Pre-sale is still a sale

In 2005, the company I founded was facing the greatest test since its inception – we were running out of money. We only had enough money to pay one-third of our staff salary. Just a few months back, we had pivoted from an education services company to an edtech company, developing interactive learning content for school teachers to use to better their teaching of biology. Our goal was to develop 30 simulations in biology, covering different topics and to sell to schools the following year. By September of 2005, we had only completed three of the 30 simulations. It was hardly enough to make any sale and to bring in much needed revenue. But we had a great product vision and road map, and these three pilot simulations showed how it would look when all 30 were completed.

So we decided to sell the three simulations we had completed.

We met with the schools and showed them the three simulations, then asked if they were willing to pre-order from us ahead of our completion of the remaining 27 and be prepared to pay in advance at a substantial discount to the launch price. More than 30 schools agreed. So we made enough revenue to tie the company through until we released the entire collection of simulations and more. This gave us the necessary financial resources to double down and to develop the next ADO that led us to a multimillion-dollar licensing contract with a partner in the region a few years later.

Even with a pilot, it is possible to generate revenue if the product is attractive to the target customer. Get the product vision right and a pre-sale is possible. With revenue secured and a steady pipeline built up, the enterprise will have the resources to grow and the credibility to raise capital from investors.

Valuing an Enterprise Based Only on Revenue may Not be Sound

Some investors can accept that price-to-revenue ratio may be a suitable metric for determining the value of scalable companies. For example, not too long ago, companies in the edtech sector have been successful in raising capital at multiples of revenue generated over the last 12 months (LTM) prior to the close of the fundraising round. Yet, not all types of revenue carry a high value.

Generally, one-off service-based revenue, such as taking on a project to develop and deliver a piece of digital content to a client without us owning the intellectual property, are less valuable than, say, one that comes from a client subscribing to a product as a service on a monthly basis. The former is non-recurring and not scalable (more projects means more people involved and more costs), while the latter is recurring (subscription on a monthly basis) and scalable (does not need to have high cost to service each subscription).

In his blog Above the Crowd,[33] Bill Gurley argued that pricing a company based on revenue may be a very crude tool for valuation, given that not all revenue is created equal. He advocates that we should look beyond revenue alone and focus on the fundamentals of the business, such as its competitive position and profitability.

Thus, we need to look at revenue growth along with two other financial metrics: gross profit margins and EBITDA margins.

Gross Profit Margins and EBITDA Margins of Scalable Ventures

Gross Profit is a financial metric that measures how profitable a business is. Gross Profit is derived from subtracting revenue from the Cost of Goods Sold (COGS):

$$Gross\ Profit = Revenue - COGS$$

COGS refers to all costs that can be directly attributed to the production and delivery of goods and services, and includes the cost of materials and labour directly involved in the production of goods and services. For example, the cost of raw materials, direct labour and manufacturing overheads that are directly tied to the production of the goods or services being sold.

33 Bill Gurley, "All Revenue is Not Created Equal: The Keys to the 10X Revenue Club" Above the Crowd (24 May 2011) <https://abovethecrowd.com/2011/05/24/all-revenue-is-not-created-equal-the-keys-to-the-10x-revenue-club/>.

Gross Profit, by itself, may not be very useful in helping us analyse the profitability performance of a business amongst its peers in the same industry. To compare the profitability with other businesses in the same industry, we use a ratio called Gross Profit Margin, which is simply dividing the gross profit by the revenue over the same period and expressing it as a percentage.

Gross Profit Margin (expressed as a percentage) =
Gross Profit/Revenue

Reid Hoffman and Chris Yeh, in their book *Blitzscaling*,[34] advocate that gross profit margin is a good indicator of how scalable a business is. They recommend that an enterprise with an ambition to scale should aim for a gross profit margin between 60 to 80 per cent.

Since the effort to sell a product may be comparable whether it's a low-margin or high-margin product, a high gross profit margin would reveal that the enterprise is able to deliver its offering at a relatively low cost to revenue. The company should therefore try to design a high-margin product as far as possible. Having a high gross profit margin also affords the company more resources (from the gross profits) to invest in better customer support and provide a better customer experience. Finally, investors tend to favour and pay a premium for companies with high gross margins as it suggests that these companies have greater cash generating power than their peers (more money is earned for the same amount of effort to sell).

The problem with just looking at gross profit margins is that we have not considered the cost of advertising and marketing, which are major contributions to the total cost of acquiring a customer or the Customer Acquisition Cost (CAC). While gross-margin numbers indicate how profitable a line of business is after it has won over a paying customer, it doesn't take into account the cost of acquiring that customer. In some industries, such as the online tutoring industry, the

---

34 Reid Hoffman & Chris Yeh, *Blitzscaling: The Lightning-Fast Path to Building Massively Valuable Companies* (HarperCollins, 2018).

CAC can be up to $3,000 per student who signs up for a $1,000 course. In this case, even with a high gross margin, the business will need to ensure that it retains this same customer for two more repeated purchases before it breaks even.

Thus, another financial metric that is very useful in tracking profitability and the scalability potential of an enterprise is the EBITDA Margin.

EBITDA Margins Tell a Different Story

Earnings Before Interest, Taxes, Depreciation and Amortisation (EBITDA) is calculated by taking a company's revenue and subtracting the COGS as well as operating expenses, such as:

- Research and development expenses;
- Sales and marketing expenses; and
- General and administrative expenses.

$$EBITDA = Revenue - Cost\ of\ Goods\ Sold\ (COGS) - Operating\ Expenses$$

[Another way to calculate EBITDA is by taking a company's operating income (EBIT) and adding back depreciation and amortisation expenses.]

While EBITDA is not recognised under Generally Accepted Accounting Principles (GAAP), it is very useful for founders and people who are evaluating an investment opportunity in addition to looking at net income, as it can provide a more accurate picture of a company's cash flow and operating performance.

With the EBITDA known, we can derive another metric called the "EBITDA margin" by dividing the EBITDA by the revenue over the same period:

$$EBITDA\ Margin\ (expressed\ as\ a\ percentage) = EBITDA/Revenue$$

The EBITDA margin is very useful in helping us to compare the profitability of a company against others in the same industry or across different industries. *For a company to be perceived as valuable and scalable, it should have an EBITDA margin of 15 per cent or higher.*

As shown in the table below, highly scalable companies tend to have EBITDA margins of at least 20 per cent. Amongst these companies, those in the social media businesses such as Meta Platforms (Facebook, Instagram) and Tencent (Wechat) tend to enjoy higher EBITDA margins of at least 30 per cent, while those in the software businesses could span a range from slightly below 20 per cent to as high as close to 50 per cent.

While online marketplace businesses tend to have lower EBITDA margins of between 10 to 20 per cent, possibly due to the costs associated with logistics and fulfilment of orders, versus the cost of delivering cloud-based solutions such as those in Salesforce.com, Microsoft and Google, successful marketplace businesses can be considered as highly scalable due to their huge user base.

Generally, companies in the retail businesses (such as Walmart, Barnes & Noble) and those that involve warehousing and heavy logistics for fulfilment (HP, Scholastic) are less scalable and have EBITDA margins that are significantly lower than 15 per cent. The outliers in this space are Apple and Amazon, both of which have diverse businesses and are heavily investing in research and development. Yet, Amazon's main business is in retailing, which is generally an extremely low-margin business. While Apple's core product is a piece of hardware, the iPhone, the company has been able to price the iPhone above its competitors because it has been able to deliver an audaciously desirable overall experience for its customers.

Company	EBITDA Margin (%)		
	2019	2020	2021
Salesforce.com	19.35	18.89	19.61
Microsoft	45.70	47.09	49.55
Alphabet (Google)	28.43	30.09	35.38
Meta Platforms	42.05	45.99	46.40
Tencent	31.46	30.66	
Alibaba	19.13	16.25	8.65
Amazon	12.95	12.47	12.60
Netflix	59.16	62.04	62.75
Disney	19.48	9.57	13.89
Apple	29.18	28.95	33.89
Hewlett Packard Enterprise (HP)	13.07	11.72	13.42
Scholastic	6.98	-1.80	8.75
Barnes & Noble Education	1.22	-7.36	-5.59
Walmart	6.18	6.11	6.35

Source of data: Macrotrends.net[35]

There are exceptions to this. In some industries, companies are able to charge sky-high prices for their products after spending an enormous amount of money in designing and manufacturing them. For example, pharmaceutical and biotechnology companies can typically spend more than $300 million to design, test and mass produce one drug before it starts to generate revenue from that product. Yet, these companies can achieve EBITDA margins that are above 30 per cent.

This is possible because pharmaceutical and biotech companies have extremely strong intellectual property protection for their discovery and inventions, mostly through patents that surround the discovery and design of each drug. These patents confer protection

---

35   "Apple EBITDA Margin 2010-2022" Macrotrends.net <https://www.macrotrends.net/stocks/charts/AAPL/apple/ebitda-margin>.

against copycats and allow them to charge super high prices for the products during the period of protection.

In other words, during the time when these patents are in force, these companies enjoy monopoly in the market for the products they own.

But to get to this stage demands a huge investment of several million dollars at the outset. As a result, such products typically originate from well-funded research institutions or the pharma-biotech companies' research teams, rather than from someone's garage as we have seen in many successful software and even hardware companies.

Company	EBITDA Margin (%)		
	2019	2020	2021
Johnson & Johnson	30.48	29.11	32.42
Pfizer	30.47	31.05	30.29
Novartis	25.49	26.64	22.11
Merck & Co	28.72	21.76	33.70
Eli Lilly	27.81	30.08	27.92

Source of data: Macrotrends.net

Thus, to achieve high EBITDA margins, we either need to charge high prices, which is possible when we have an ADO that can be protected against competition, or we can be highly scalable, moving quickly on a solid business model to gain a competitive advantage and a large user base with an ADO that is sticky and novel.

Burn before We Earn or Earn to Burn?

If an enterprise is EBITDA negative, it suggests that the enterprise is still finding its way to profitability, even if its revenue may be stellar. The enterprise is still burning more cash than it can earn.

Burn Multiples Indicate when to Start Cutting Cost

David Sacks, in his blog, discussed how the burn multiple can measure the capital efficiency of a startup and when a founder should look at cutting costs.[36] A burn multiple of a business is calculated by dividing the amount of money it burns over a period of, say, one year or one month, by the amount of recurring revenue it brings in over the same period:

Burn Multiple (BM) = Cash Burn/Recurring Revenue (ARR, MRR)

If:
BM > 1, it means that the company is spending more cash than it is generating;
BM = 1, the company is breaking even; and
BM < 1, it means the company is generating more cash than it burns.

Sacks recommended that for venture-staged companies, a burn multiple of more than two calls for suspicion that the startup isn't managing its capital efficiently while any burn multiple above a score of three doesn't paint a good picture and demands action from founders to correct the course.

Taking together what I have discussed earlier in this chapter, if the burn multiple of an enterprise is > 1, it already means that the enterprise isn't generating an EBITDA, let alone considering if it is reaching the target EBITDA margin to make it scalable. This is to be expected in a venture at the early stages of its growth, when the venture is trying to find that elusive product-market fit and has probably just launched the MVP.

But this shouldn't be allowed to drag for too long. If this goes on for, say, a few more months, then the founder should quickly evaluate if this is a problem with:

36   David Sacks, "The Burn Multiple – How Startups Should Think About Capital Efficiency" Medium (24 April 2020) <https://medium.com/craft-ventures/the-burn-multiple-51a7e43cb200>.

- Too high a COGS, leading to low gross margins;
- Too high a CAC, suggesting a problem with sales efficiency; or
- Too high a churn, which may be corroborated by a low NPS, suggesting that the product isn't sticky enough.

The exception may be when a startup is building something that has a high level of market protection such as a piece of killer tech that will wipe out the competition or a patent that establishes a super high barrier to entry (we see that in pharmaceutical startups on route to getting a patent on a drug formulation that could be worth millions in licensing revenue alone after it's been developed). In this instance, we may be able to tolerate a longer period of positive high burn multiple for the startup. But a prudent founder operating in a small or a fragmented market would have to ask just how long the new venture be allowed to go on like this before it becomes desperate for a cash injection. In other words, how much money does the company have in its bank account before its runway runs out and the founders risk losing the company to a predatory investor who injects new money into the company (see Chapter 10 "The Exit – Sell, Float or Close")?

And in the meantime, what can a founder do to mitigate the chances of getting into high burn multiples before it's too late?

Mitigate Burn by Having the Machinery Ready from Day 1
A new venture needs to validate its narrative in as short a time as possible. It needs to test its hypothesis for a business problem and the role its solution can play in solving the problem. It needs to launch fast, test fast, fail fast and learn fast. These days, having to burn a whole lot of cash to launch and test a prototype in the market isn't going to cut it for the founder and the investors. To avoid running out of cash prematurely, we need to *have the machinery in place on Day 1 and be ready to launch by Month 2.*

Depending on the nature and type of business, the machinery can take different forms. For a human resources tech and talent management business, it could take the form of a software platform that organises and analyses candidates' and employers' input for better qualification and placement of job applicants. In a meal delivery business, it could be the central kitchen with its in-house chef and a food delivery rider network. In an online tutoring business, it could be a live-tutoring platform and the software technology for content management.

These days, the technologies that power these machinery components are readily available from different parts of the world and can be procured or licensed from providers. These parties are very willing to take their brands out of the mix, allowing us to brand the product any which way we prefer. Should we wish to develop the tech ourselves without having to maintain a sizable workforce, we can partner talent management vendors that can help us curate, assemble and manage very capable experts, whom we can subcontract out to the development of the software to our specifications, at a fraction of the cost and with a lot less headache than if we were to do it ourselves. We just need to look hard and far enough to find the right vendors to partner with.

While the inability to own an underlying piece of technology could be frowned upon by investors, there is merit to this method, especially in the early stages of a venture.

Having our eyes on this target systemically impacts the strategy of a venture at the point of inception. It forces the founders to maximise their resources to beg, borrow and deal with potential partners to get the machinery in place so they can launch the venture by the second month.

Check out Chapter 6 "Bootstrapping – Beg, Borrow, Build, Deal" and Chapter 8 "Going to Market" for ideas on how to do this at low cost and high speed.

Profitable Enterprises Fetch Higher Value in the Current Climate

Circling back to how some investors may look at revenue multiples to price companies, using the edtech investment landscape as an example, one could argue that this way of pricing a company is valid since edtech is a high-gross margins business. While this may be true, it is just as important to look at the EBITDA margins of a company to get a more complete picture of the enterprise. Where possible, founders should grow their companies to embody these attributes:

- Fast revenue growth of at least a few folds year-on-year;
- Positive EBITDA with EBITDA margins at more than 15 per cent; and
- High gross margins.

These financial metrics speak volumes for the growth potential of the enterprise and the ability of its management to manage the fiscal risks associated with operating in these volatile times.

In my conversations with a fund manager, he told me that given the economic climate these days, and for the moment, his focus is on "companies that are profitable and growing. They don't have to be an established company. They can even be a startup. As long as they can show that they are profitable and are growing, they are investable in my book." I think this sums it all up for those of us who are building a business to raise capital for growth.

Focus on the right things and use the right metrics to monitor your venture performance, and you will get the financial support that you need.

SECTION 3
THE EXECUTION

6

Bootstrapping
Beg, Borrow, Build, Deal

"If I invest $100,000 in your company, would you be prepared to not take a salary for the next 18 months?" – This was the challenge that an angel investor put to a founder of a pre-revenue startup.

The angel investor, who has built a very successful company with multiple offices in the region and has personally invested in and exited several startups, went on to elaborate: "I need to know that you are prepared to put it all on the line to make this venture work. As an entrepreneur myself, I hold this principle very dear to me and it has served me well."

Sounds cruel, right?

As an entrepreneur and an investor myself, I can see the wisdom behind this demand from the investor.

But I certainly do not agree with my angel investor friend that the founder takes nothing home for such a long period of time. We want experienced and qualified founders for a startup because we want the startup to grow fast enough for an exit in 36 months. And these individuals are not likely to be 20-something-year-old upstarts who are keen to change their world from the dormitory of their university or the basement of their parents' home. There are exceptions, of course, but I would expect many of such qualified founders to have already reached a certain age and have worked for quite a few years, building a solid network and domain expertise. These individuals would have families, probably a mortgage and might even be recovering from a failed business in the past. So they need at least some basic income to make ends meet or they will always be looking for side gigs to bring home the bread for their family. That kind of commitment dilution at the start isn't good for any venture.

Yet, I feel jitterish when a founder comes to me with a nice idea and a beautiful deck for his business, and expects me to fund him just on that, when he hasn't proven in any way to suggest that the business is promising enough to be investable by a third party. To me, expecting someone else to build your dream when you're not prepared to put it all on the line is unfair to the investor and doesn't bode well for you as the founder.

You need to first make it work to a point where you can convincingly tell an investor that your business is for real, and that it can help the investor make really good money in the foreseeable future.

"But then, without the seed capital, how can this even start?" quipped one fund manager.

"The founding team will just need to bootstrap – get the right people to come together and get the business up and running first," was my response.

In this chapter, we explore the different groups of people and organisations we can bring on board to help the founders get their new venture off the ground to at least test out the idea, all done at low to zero upfront cost. These groups of *founding helpers* may present themselves in different forms, such as the core founding team members, the cheerleaders, the borrowed folks and the alliance partners.

But first, let's discuss why I prefer to bootstrap than to raise money at the outset, even if I may have investors who are prepared to write cheques to invest through various financial instruments that may not immediately carve out from the founder some equity and control of the company.

Never Sell Ourselves Short without First Testing Our Narrative

It is tempting for new venture founders to raise some startup investment from third-party angel investors or venture capitalists before the venture even opens its doors for business. Some entrepreneurs have been able to do that quite elegantly but, generally, I don't recommend it.

Unless the founder is a larger-than-life entrepreneur or has an excellent network of investors who believe the founder for what he or she says about the enterprise, maybe because of a successful exit in a previous venture, investors will tend to want a large chunk of the company for the money they are prepared to put in at this early stage of the venture. The shares of a pre-revenue, pre-product company without a clear path to revenue or profitability are generally the cheapest. Some investors may agree to structure the investment as a loan that is converted into the company's shares later on, but these days, those who agree to do so without fairly onerous conditions are few and far between.

So, I would recommend that founders wait until the enterprise has gotten some quick wins, whether in the form of a customer contract, or some validation that the business model will generate revenue in the very near future, before raising money from people whom they don't know well. In the meantime, try to bootstrap by tapping on the resources that I will be discussing in this chapter. And if money is still needed, find ways to borrow from friends and family, who tend to give friendlier terms.

Bootstrap Resource #1: The Core Team
Steve Jobs Wouldn't have Been Able to Build Apple on His Own

Apple co-founder Steve Jobs was a visionary quite unlike any other. He imagined how the world would look like with a touchscreen mobile device that could be operated with just our fingers and presented the iPhone. He envisioned how a singular closed ecosystem could serve the users of Apple products better than an open, fragmented one. And he was right. He championed the Apple store as a place for customers to experience, learn and service Apple products. But he couldn't have done it without the help of Steve Wozniak, who built the first Apple computer, or Tim Cook, a master of logistics and operations, or Jony Ive, whose clean design got his attention, or a team of unsung developers behind the iPhone keyboard and the Safari browser that was to be the fastest internet browser the world had ever seen. A visionary who can envision the road map for an enterprise remains one who only dreams, if he is not backed up by those who can build and operate his vision.

A Startup Must Possess Five Essential Abilities from the Start

<u>Design</u>: this refers to the ability to design a business that solves a big enough problem in an audaciously desirable way. It is the ingredient that can make a venture offering catch on quickly, gain users and generate revenue in a short period of time (aka *traction*). The designer goes beyond simply designing a product or a service but considers the entire value chain within which the business operates, before structuring business models to target each customer group in different parts of the value chain. Designers need to have an intimate understanding of the target customer's problems, deep domain knowledge and an incredible imagination to craft and present a solution that can make the customer rush to adopt it.

<u>Grow</u>: the ability to see far enough on how the world will change and to get the team on board to steer the enterprise on a course to meet that change. As venture builders, growers are able to see who to partner with, where to get fresh funds, and how to exit, selling this vision to the right people, whether they be customers, distributors, partners or investors. This is what it means to grow an enterprise. It

calls for an ability to envision the future, take a design that can meet this future demand and communicate the vision to stakeholders to get their buy-in. In many instances, the ability to grow and to design may rest on the same person.

Build: the ability to build a product that is sticky and has high perceived value is critical to the success of any venture. Builders in the venture need to work closely with the designers to ensure that whatever is built in the "factory" fits the design narrative, enabling the sellers to get customers to commit to the sale, and the growers to build on the growth story of the enterprise. Depending on the nature of the business, builders could be operators of central kitchens (for meal delivery businesses), coders (for online tech businesses) or owners of membership databases (for platform businesses).

Sell: the ability to sell is not limited to individuals who do door-to-door sales. Sellers should possess a solid network that enables unprecedented access to customers to test the Minimum Viable Product (MVP), make tweaks to it over different iterations to find the right fit or to ditch the MVP for something else. Sellers are also domain experts in marketing analytics, able to dive deep into key data points such as the Net Promoter Score (NPS) and other related metrics to assess the viability of the product as a growth candidate for the enterprise.

Operate: the ability to orchestrate the business and operations processes needed to ensure anything that is designed gets built and sold. Operators string all functional aspects of the business together to ensure that the enterprise meets its goals, for the growers to build an exciting narrative towards an eventual exit.

Each ability could rest on one individual or some individuals may be gifted to possess more abilities. In some businesses, a single founder may possess all five abilities, but these are rare situations and if it does happen, it's usually temporary. The trick in building a new venture in its starting phases is to find people or parties who, when put together, enable the enterprise to possess all five abilities to get the job done, and the business up and running as quickly and as efficiently as possible.

My second venture started as a company of one

I started my second venture to provide life sciences enrichment services to schools in Singapore. I figured that since I had domain expertise in this area and am gifted with the ability to simplify complex knowledge for people in an engaging manner, I could build a business around these two domains. I had also picked up some graphic design skills during my university days, so I could design some nice brochures and lesson materials for my customers and their students. In my previous job as a management consultant, I also learned how to financially model a business and I was quite good with numbers, despite my background in biology.

I started this new venture in my bedroom and a typical day would consist of printing the brochures to be mailed out, taking the public bus to a nearby stationery store to get the brochures properly bound and laminated, then walking to the post office to get them mailed out to prospective clients. I would then take a break for lunch, before either returning home to call prospective customers or going to their schools to meet and pitch the offering. I would then go home to write follow-up emails and design the lesson materials. This continued until I made my first $50,000 in revenue before I started recruiting new members to join my team, operating my first office from my home before moving to a proper office.

I was fortunate enough to have the abilities that enabled me to start things off for my new venture. But that didn't last long. Soon after, revenue started picking up rapidly and new demands on the subject matter arose. I realised that what I knew wasn't enough for the company to meet those demands. So I recruited more domain experts to join me in order to offer a wider repertoire of products to the target customers. Some of them also doubled up to sell our offerings to more customers, expanding our revenue and customer base.

Because I had next to zero technical knowledge in coding, when I started the next venture in education technology, I needed to find more people with complementary abilities to join my team. Those individuals brought with them expertise that could help us develop some really great cloud-based solutions, and they had the network to help us rapidly expand our developing teams to nearby countries, saving the company an incredible amount of money in research and development.

Start with a Team

Over lunch, a senior executive of one leading venture capital firm in Singapore shared with me that her team, along with other investors, often had the problem of assessing whether a startup has the right mix of talent to survive and grow in the early stages, which are typically the riskiest time for a new venture. Quite often, many tech startups already have a promising product that is developed by the founders. I told this executive that I would focus my attention on the people who are driving sales in the company since "revenue solves all problems".

"The CEO, who is the main founder, told us that he is very confident in getting sales for the company, and he has started to do that. That's enough, no?" We discussed this and felt that this wasn't a good thing. The main founder was already the chief designer and visionary of the company, and being the main seller as well would suggest an arbitrary limit to the revenue potential of the company. After all, how much can one person do without neglecting the other functions?

In some rare and fortunate cases, a founder may be able to hold multiple functions in an enterprise, but this rarely lasts. And once the enterprise reaches a point where it needs fresh capital from investors, the burden of performing the different functions – from selling to designing to operating the business – should be spread over a few key people in the organisation.

In the starting phases of any new venture, money is a rare commodity. So, we need to find like-minded individuals who possess complementary abilities to join us as co-founders. Working as a team, each co-founder will have a share in the new venture and is responsible for the success and failure of the enterprise. When the new venture takes the form of a company, co-founders become shareholders. Prior to that, some co-founders may opt to operate as a loose alliance that is described in an agreement that everyone enters into.

So, when investors evaluate if a new venture has what it takes in the team to make it work, what do they look out for in the individuals that make up the team to assess if they have what it takes to serve those functions?

What Investors Look for in the Bootstrap Team

I have discussed earlier the abilities of a founding team often determine the likelihood of success of the new venture. But abilities are often contextual and are not apparent at first glance to an outsider. So, potential investors would want to look at something more to qualify the founding team for the job. I can distil that down to two "priors", prior experience and prior track record:

1. Prior Experience – Where I have worked before

Where we have worked prior to starting our venture says a lot about the skills that we may have picked up. For example, if we have worked in one of the world's top consulting firms after we left school, we are saying that we have skills in analysing and modelling opportunities, as well as communicating the opportunities to stakeholders. The table below is a sample of what our previous work experience may say about us.

Where we have worked prior to setting up this venture	What it says about what we know	Why it matters
As a teacher in a school.	We know methods of instruction and management of students as well as operations related to an education setting.	If our venture is an education-centred or an edtech one, then domain knowledge in education is always preferred.
As a civil servant in the healthcare industry.	We know the inner workings of the civil service and the healthcare industry.	If our venture deals with government contracts, then this prior experience will help us as it suggests that we may have the network to sniff out trends and potential projects in the future, and the know-how to approach the relevant stakeholders to bid for these projects.
As an entrepreneur who failed in his previous business.	We know about what it takes to start something from scratch and operate it (up to the point of either failing or being kicked out of our venture).	Investors like a "recycled" entrepreneur – someone who has been there and, most importantly, learned important lessons from mistakes to not ever make them again. A famous example of such an entrepreneur is Adam Neumann, the founder of WeWork, who was ousted in 2019 and then staged a comeback in 2022 with another venture called Flow, which raised $350 million from Andreessen Horowitz, one of the most prominent venture capitalists in the US.[37]

37   Andrew Ross Sorkin et al., "Adam Neumann Gets a New Backer" *The New York Times* (15 August 2022) <https://www.nytimes.com/2022/08/15/business/dealbook/adam-neumann-flow-new-company-wework-real-estate.html>.

2. <u>Prior Track Record – What I have done before</u>

This is a key piece of information and the founder would be wise to think carefully about how to share this with potential investors. By presenting the track record of each team member, the founder is saying that he or she has thought through carefully who to bring on board in the starting line-up of the venture. When presenting the track record of a team, consider what each member has done and how he or she would fit into any one or more of the five essential abilities that I have listed earlier in this section.

When it comes to the founder, there is no better track record than to say that he or she has been through at least one round of starting a venture, and better still, exiting it, even if the exit value wasn't anything to shout about. The fact that a founder has such a "full-circle experience" of starting, growing and exiting a business checks a lot of boxes for an investor when thinking about whether the founder has the necessary abilities to start and operate a successful venture. Even if the founder didn't get to exit the previous venture and might have even been ousted from the venture, as we have seen in the case of WeWork's founder, Adam Neumann, investors may still view such experience in very good light, to the point of writing multimillion-dollar cheques on an enterprise that hasn't even opened its doors for business. We saw this in August 2022, when *The New York Times* reported that Marc Andreesen of Andreesen Horowitz , who invested $350 million into Neumann's startup, Flow, wrote in a blog post that "we love seeing repeat-founders build on past successes by growing from lessons learned." Where Neumann was concerned, he added that "the successes and lessons are plenty".

But what if we are unable to find such individuals to join our team as co-founders and agree to work for little to no salary in the beginning stages? We could turn to our cheerleaders, borrowed folks and alliances for help.

Bootstrap Resource #2: The Cheerleaders

Cheerleaders are people or organisations who root for us on the sidelines and introduce their friends to work with us. They don't play an active role in advising us on how to steer our business towards success but they may tell their friends about us. And if their friends are potential customers, we could score some contracts. Cheerleaders are typically our shareholders or investors, and they can even be our clients who bring us to more clients in their ecosystem. Cheerleaders do not demand to be remunerated and they help us mainly because they are probably already users of our products and are loving the experience of being associated with us. Ironically, we can gain many new cheerleaders for our business through excellent customer recovery as a result of hiccups in our interaction with them. Thus, having a solid customer recovery process and being totally committed to the customer (which includes learning how to say "no" to some customers' requests while still winning their hearts) is a key requirement of a successful go-to-market strategy. In the next chapter, Chapter 7 "Know Your Customer, Love Your Customer", I discuss the importance of the customer recovery process in helping us to cement a solid relationship with our customers.

Bootstrap Resource #3: The Borrowed Folks

The founding emperor of the ancient Han dynasty in China, Liu Bang (刘邦), wasn't known for being a tactical genius, a mighty warrior or an inspiring leader whose words could scale mountains. In fact, historical writings seem to suggest that he was a philanderer and a person with little ambition. He was, however, supported by a team of loyal subjects who were his childhood friends and a few highly able generals who helped him win battles and escape death plots. And he had the help of an incredibly wise and shrewd advisor in the form of Zhang Liang (张良), who taught him how to escape unscathed from the famous Hongmen Feast (鸿门宴) that his enemy had set up to kill him. Zhang Liang also helped Liu Bang recruit the general Han Xun, who eventually led Liu's army to defeat the enemy and unite China again, starting the Han Dynasty that lasted for approximately 400 years.

Here's the catch: Zhang Liang wasn't an employee or subject of Liu Bang. In fact, he wasn't even an associate of Liu, nor did he derive any official posts or remuneration from Liu prior to the founding of the Han dynasty. His boss at that time was the emperor of the Qi state in what we now know as the Shangdong Province in China. It was only after the founding of the Han dynasty that Zhang Liang held high ranking positions in the imperial court and served as a subject of Liu Bang.

Zhang Liang is a borrowed folk.

He is the guy who doesn't belong to our official payroll, has a day job elsewhere but plays an instrumental role in the success of our enterprise, often by being the key strategist behind the scenes, and by helping us connect to important people and resources that could make or break our venture.

Borrowed folks are those who do not belong to our team but have a stake in our cause to fight for us, sometimes using their own army and resources. They take many forms, such as an organisation that licences its tech to us at a really low cost or for nominal equity in our company, or consultants who possess unique and strategic qualities to help us plot, plan and execute our business. They don't run our operations but can introduce us to those who can, if we need it. And they know people who can help us grow our revenue at much higher speeds than if we were to do it ourselves.

We typically reward borrowed folks with a mix of commission on a success basis, shares in the company and monthly retainers, depending on the involvement of the parties.

Bootstrap Resource #4: The Alliance

"Long shots aren't usually as long as they seem."
Robert Iger, *The Ride of a Lifetime*[38]

---

38 Robert Iger, *The Ride of a Lifetime – Lessons learned from 15 years as CEO of the Walt Disney Company* (Random House, 2019), p 191.

Apple's Steve Jobs disliked Disney. A lot. That was until Robert (Bob) Iger assumed the role of Disney's CEO. In his memoir, *The Ride of a Lifetime*, Bob Iger recounted how he got back to being on talking terms with Jobs who, at that time, had deep-rooted animosity towards Disney. Iger wanted Disney to acquire Pixar Animation Studios and felt that this deal would help turn Disney around. Disney Animation had, by then, wane in relevance, having lost nearly $400 million over the past decade. An acquisition of Pixar would turn Disney animation around, from a lacklustre, past-its-prime player to the world's leading animation house.

The problem: Steve Jobs was the majority shareholder of Pixar and many thought he would never sell Pixar to Disney, given the misgivings both had for each other. So how did Iger get Jobs to the table and make the deal?

Through an alliance between Disney and Apple based on a deal that was totally unrelated to Pixar, and the following was how Iger did it.

Iger first told Jobs that he had all his music stored in his iPod, to show how much he admired the ecosystem that Apple had in place for music. Iger then offered Disney's shows on a TV version of iTunes that Apple could set up. Incidentally, Apple was working on a similar idea and having Disney's content would certainly have helped. Five months after these two industry legends agreed to collaborate, Apple launched the TV version of iTunes, with five Disney shows available for download. With an alliance in place and the lines now open, Iger proceeded to discuss with Jobs the prospect of Disney acquiring Pixar. Disney acquired Pixar in 2006 for $7.4 billion.

Steve Jobs wasn't the easiest of executives to deal with, and this was common knowledge. Drew Houston, the founder of DropBox, had told Business Insider in 2017 that prior to his meeting with Jobs, he had talked to a bunch of his friends, and said that "the stories fell squarely in two categories: you either got Chill Steve or Very Mean Steve, so we didn't know which one we were gonna get."[39]

---

39   Libby Kane, CFEI & Alyson Shontell, "'You either got Chill Steve or Very Mean Steve': Dropbox founder remembers being summoned to Apple by Steve Jobs – then told his startup would be killed" Business Insider (15 June 2017) < https://www.businessinsider.com/drew-houston-dropbox-steve-jobs-2017-6>.

Yet, Bob Iger could turn Steve Jobs around and convinced him to agree to sell Pixar to Disney. Iger was able to do that as he was well aware of Jobs' obsession to build the best experience on Apple's mobile devices through iTunes, and how Disney could feature in that plan. Disney had content. Very good content. Apple had a thriving ecosystem that was hungry for more content in more varied forms. There was a fit. But that was not Iger's ultimate goal: Iger wanted Pixar, and figured that throwing up something that Jobs wanted could open the door to discussion of the matter. And it did.

A good alliance can help any business to get into a new market or offer a service to a totally different niche, and it can be a stepping stone to something much bigger, often without much cost upfront. Generally, the more stable alliances have the following characteristics:

- Both companies are in very different and almost non-overlapping industries, even if they are targeting the same customer, and both are really good at what they do. In the Disney-Apple case, Disney is in the content business while Apple is in the device and media ecosystem business. Both companies are leaders in their field and did not see themselves going to each other's domain in the near future.
- Both want something from the other: Apple needed good content to accompany its launch of the video offering on iTunes while Disney, well, it wanted to use this as a springboard to acquire Pixar.
- While both are strong players in their respective fields, it usually takes one party to eat humble pie and court the other at the start. Knowing Jobs' personality, and being ready to talk terms with Jobs about Pixar, Iger was prepared to take the lower seat in the dynamics between them.

The commercial structures surrounding alliances can take many forms, the most straightforward being a share of revenue that is derived from the alliance business.

When looking to form an alliance with another party, first find out what the other party really wants and which we have, then use that as a point of alignment with them. A good alliance is very rewarding, but remember any alliance can be fragile, especially if the leverage is skewed towards one particular party.

The right alliance can complete a service

The electric vehicle (EV) is set to change the way we travel and buy personal vehicles. These EVs are smooth, quiet and they pick up speed much quicker than most petrol-powered vehicles, not to mention that they are friendly to the environment. But they are expensive, costing as much as 50 per cent more than their petrol cousins, and it is a pain to get the battery charged, especially if you live in an apartment with no charging point in the estate.

So a startup in Singapore has offered a mobile power charging service for EV drivers to summon a mobile charging station to a location of their choice to charge the car battery, if they do not have access to a permanent charging point.[40] To reach its target users, this company would partner with distributors of EVs in Singapore, forming an alliance that enables the car distributors to offer an additional service that completes the customer's user experience.

Do all EV owners need this service?

"Possibly, but not likely," according to a mutual friend who purchased an EV recently.

She continues, "It seems that most customers have already figured out the routine to charge their vehicles and don't need to use that service very much. But to know that this service is always available (for emergencies) is a great feature to have."

Not All Resources Cost Lots of Money

The examples presented in this chapter are just some of the ways founders of new ventures can gain access to technology, expertise, markets and

40   Lee Nian Tjoe, "Singapore firm offers mobile charging service for electric vehicles" *The Straits Times* (7 June 2022) <https://www.straitstimes.com/singapore/transport/first-mobile-fast-charging-service-for-electric-vehicles-in-singapore>.

network without having to spend crazy amounts of money on marketing and recruiting only the top talent. As new venture champions, we should find creative ways to sell our vision to potential partners and get their buy-in to the point where they are prepared to journey with us despite suffering some economic losses in the starting stages.

And some good and talented people really do look beyond monetary benefits when deciding whether to join a small company or a startup, as can be seen in a former staff of my previous venture, who recalled on LinkedIn how I had asked him to join me and his experience of working with me as his CEO:

> When my former CEO was convincing me to join his firm, he was aware that I was considering other options.
>
> During our third meeting, he said,
>
> "▨▨▨▨, I know we will not be able to match what you are going to get in terms of compensation in bigger organisations.
>
> However, if you do join us, you will be helping to make a huge impact in the world of education by disrupting how kids learn STEM. You will also get a front-row seat working with the CEO as he leads and drives the company forward."
>
> He was true to his word.
>
> The two years spent in the Edutech company he founded was one of the most exhilarating and rewarding periods of my career.
>
> Not only did I get to do the HR work such as culture building and engagement, but by working alongside a visionary and purpose-driven CEO, I also got to pick up valuable insights on leadership, vision and strategy, problem-solving, and entrepreneurship.
>
> When it comes to joining a new company, compensation is certainly important, but it is not everything. It's also important to consider other factors such as:
> ☑ Leadership
> ☑ Culture
> ☑ Opportunities to learn and grow
> ☑ Team and collaboration
> ☑ Impact that you would be making.
>
> Agree?
>
> What do you look for when you join a company, my friends?

So, find the right motivation that will move our partners to come on board and we can beg, borrow, build and deal to start us off in any new venture.

7

Know Your Customer, Love Your Customer

Who is Our Customer?

Many of us are probably familiar with the acronyms B2B, B2C, D2C and C2C, which are commonly used to describe the nature of a business by means of the customer it serves:

- B2B means "business-to-business", a model by which a business sells its products to another business;
- B2C means "business-to-consumer", where a business sells its products to the end user (the consumer), sometimes through an intermediary such as a retail store;
- D2C means "direct-to-consumer", where the end user buys directly from the business that makes the product, usually via the business's own website or from an online marketplace; and
- C2C means "consumer-to-consumer", where a consumer sells to another consumer.

Knowing which category our business belongs to can help us know who our customers are.

Let's use an example of a hypothetical company that manufactures and sells a brand of hair shampoo called Brilliant Shine. This company manufacturing Brilliant Shine (the first "B") needs to first sell the product to a distributor (the second "B"), who in turn would sell to a store (the third "B") or the hair salon (the fourth "B"), and the store would then sell to the end user ("C").

In this chain, Brilliant Shine's manufacturer can be considered to be in the business-to-business (B2B) business, since its customer is another business. Going down the chain, the other players could either be a B2B or a business-to-consumer (B2C) business. If they sell to a retailer, who in turn sells to the end user, then they are in a B2C business, despite the retailer being between the manufacturer and the end user. If they sell directly to the consumer, possibly through their website, or they own a shop in a mall to sell Brilliant Shine, or they sell it through an online shopping marketplace, then they can be considered to be in the direct-to-consumer (D2C) business.

There are many different iterations of this model and increasingly, it can be hard to categorise clearly if a business is B2B, B2C or D2C. But the point of doing this exercise is to know clearly just who is the buyer of one's products and services, and if they do so with the intention of reselling them to someone downstream. Having a clear understanding of the ecosystem in which our products and services flow through and are used will help us to craft a powerful go-to-market strategy.

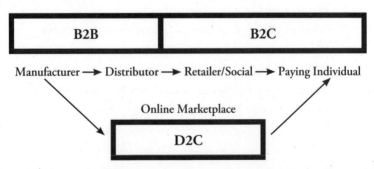

Working the ecosystem to products by the trainloads

My friend used to be one of the top salespersons in one of the world's leading consumer product companies when he retired before the age of 40. I once asked him how he managed to sell products by the trainloads given that his business was largely B2B, selling to a distributor in bulk.

"I needed to find the people who will buy from my customers. Once I have established this flow of goods, it is easy to sell in bulk to my customers since they know who to sell to next," he explained plainly.

Several years ago, when shopping for a new car, the car sales agent offered to take in my old car at a good price to reduce the friction of me buying a new car from him. He later told me that he is able to do so while pitching the sale to me because he already has a network of used car dealers who can take in my car as part of the deal.

When we know who our buyer is and what can trigger a purchase, and if we are able to work the ecosystem through which the relevant goods will flow, we can make the sale and generate the revenue.

What does Our Customer Look Like?

To be able to offer something audaciously desirable to our customer, we need to have an intimate knowledge of who this customer is, what are his or her needs and wants, what jobs he or she needs to get done on a daily, monthly, annual or even hourly basis. If the customer is a business, then we need to have deep knowledge of the nature of this customer's business, where this customer fits in the value chain and the ecosystem, and what are the pain points, just to name a few pieces of information that will be useful to us.

I find it useful to profile our target customers in order to give a tangible picture of the party that we will be selling to and whose problems we are trying to solve. This goes beyond looking at the obvious needs of the customer, such as making a profit for a corporate customer (a "B"), or getting good results for a schooling child (a "C").

We need to delve deeper to find out about the wants of that customer and to answer this critical question: "When we present (our product) to the customer, what will bring about a delight in the customer quite unlike any other experience?"

Here are some useful questions we can ask to construct the customer's profile and evaluate the relevance of our product to the target customer.

If the Target Customer is	
An Individual Consumer (C)	**A Company or Another Organisation (B)**
Is this individual (C) the payor, the user or both?	Is this company (B) using our product or reselling it, whether as a whole or as part of a bigger offering?
Who is C paying for? For example, for children's learning products, the C could be the parent while the user is the child under the parent's care.	What business is B in? What does it do and who are its customers?
	How many people does it employ?
What is C's daily routine like?	What is the vision and mission of B?
What are C's interests and aspirations? Where does our product fit in with these?	What does a typical sales and delivery cycle look like for B? (Try to get as much information as the prospect can disclose.)
Which income bracket does C belong to?	What operational problems or grievances is B going through that you have heard from the company's contact?
How much would C spend on a daily or monthly basis? Spent on what?	
	What is the decision-making culture of B? For example, is it a top-down culture or a bottom-up one?
	Are there specific people in B who are highly influential, even if they may not be directly involved in the project that you may be pitching for? What can you find out about those individuals or groups?

Relevance of our product

For the individual customer:

- Where in this routine did the customer encounter problems that our solution can solve?
- How does our product help the customer reach his or her aspirations?
- What would make the customer want to cancel any subscriptions with us?

For the company/corporate customer:

- Who in the company uses our product (be as specific as possible)? How does using this product help this person?
- When does the company use our product? How often is this being used and for what purpose?
- What is the vision of success when using our product? What is the company trying to achieve with our product? Why is this important?
- What are we replacing with our product? What does the company need to do to replace us in the following year? Is it hard for them to replace us?

Love Thy Customer

A friend of mine recently shared his experience of buying a gaming chair – the ones that look very much like an ordinary desk swivel chair except it is designed with curves to ensure good posture. And it costs an arm and a leg. He told us that shortly after he bought the chair, he received a call from the company, asking for his time to let them find out more about the reasons behind his purchase. That conversation ended with him directly talking to the CEO of the company on his purchase decision, experience and pain points. It lasted more than 30 minutes. And he appreciated the gesture from the leadership of this company.

Clearly this company demonstrated love for its customers and wanted to know what made the customers choose its brand of chairs over those of its competitors. It doesn't matter if our customer is an individual, another business or a non-profit organisation – once we learn to love our customers and understand their pain points, we would not be far off from making them love us back to spread the word about just how awesome we are. And we should be able to track these reciprocal loves as I will discuss further in this chapter.

Sell What Customers Want, Not Just What They Need

We discussed at length earlier about the importance of identifying the problems that really matter to the customer. The customer can usually see what he or she needs but rarely knows what he/she wants, until we show it to them. They depend on the clever vendor to provide them with a vision that they haven't thought of but are incredibly drawn to when it can be seen clearly – this is the core idea behind an audaciously desirable service or product (Chapter 2 "Present the Audaciously Desirable").

Let's take the example of Taobao, an online marketplace in China. Taobao is designed to serve Chinese-speaking customers and everything about this app says so – it's all in Chinese and the app design fits the Chinese culture. Then there is a big challenge of learning to make shipping arrangements self-service style to ensure that you get what you have ordered in the cheapest possible way. Despite all the barriers to adoption, more and more users are getting on board the app, and some actually know very little of the Chinese language. If it is so difficult to use (high friction), then why are people outside of China still picking up the app for their online shopping fix?

To answer this question, we need to dive into the psyche of an online shopper. At the core, the shopper needs to be sure that the ordered items will be delivered safely to him/her. But beyond this, the shopper wants diversity and low prices. And Taobao delivers just that. The platform boasts some of the widest ranges of goods available anywhere. Users are spoilt for choice as the platform curates products from its online stores in China, the manufacturing hub of the world. If a user sees something of interest in a physical store, he or she only needs to use the app to take a picture of that item and, within seconds, the page on the app will be populated with items that either look similar or are identical to the one just seen in the physical store.

And the prize: most of these items are probably priced at a fraction of the retail price.

Recently, a friend of mine told me that she has been invited by another friend to lunch so she can coach this friend on how to use Taobao. My friend is essentially providing the kind of service to her friend similar to the type that the Apple Store would provide to its customers, except that in this case, this is being done by a user for another user. That's product promotion at its finest.

Consider the following products and services against what the customers may want:

If you are in the business of ...	What you think may be the main focus of your offering	What your customers may want in addition
Operating a fine dining restaurant	The best tasting food	The whole experience of dining, from food presentation to the attention of the servers, to the pacing of the food and everything else that makes the experience a special and memorable one.
Top tier business programme	The curriculum and the lecturers	The network with a distinguished alumni.
Short term rental of apartments	Having clean apartments and making the reservation process easy.	The entire experience of soaking up the culture of the community in every place they visit.

Customers tend to buy more of what they want than what they need. So, sell what customers want but make sure that what they need is already taken care of.

Often, delivering what the customer wants goes beyond simply providing a particular product or a service to knowing *how* to deliver that offering, providing a comprehensive and total customer experience that the customer desires.

Provide a Total Experience for the Customer

Apple excels in being the world's leading computer company, producing computing devices that are intuitively easy to use for the common folk, complete with a powerful ecosystem that connects different devices and lets its customers get access to loads of content by third party providers. Most of the features of the latest models are beautifully displayed online, with the website clearly showing the features of each model and comparing it to the other models. Orders for any device can be made online to be delivered to the location specified by the customer. Apple has also delegated some of the retail services to approved resellers while a handful of approved service agents are authorised by Apple to conduct servicing and repair services. So, it looks like Apple has gotten it covered in terms of the easy use of the products it offers and the places to go to get them fixed. So why the need for the Apple Store?

Convenience.

The Apple Store provides customers with a convenient and easy way to learn about and get the most out of their Apple products through product showcases and workshops. The store also offers services such as technical support for the customer who encounters difficulty or needs expert attention on the product.

While we have not seen such attention to pre and post-sale of computing and mobile devices from other brands, Apple provides a total customer experience with the Apple Store, from viewing to purchasing, using, servicing and repairing of all Apple products. Apple sees that its encounter with the customer does not stop at getting the product into the customer's hands but continues on the journey with this product throughout its lifespan. In fact, the store is so important to the total customer experience strategy that it could be the reason for Steve Jobs appointing Millard Drexler, who was the CEO of The Gap, as a member of Apple's board of directors from 1999 to 2016, possibly because of Drexler's expertise in retail and merchandising, given his experience in leading The Gap, a highly successful retail chain in the

US. This strategy has proven effective in setting Apple apart from its competitors, enabling it to provide its customers with what they want and not just what they need. Who would have thought that mobile devices and their owners require such tender loving care?

Taobao is another example of a platform that provides a total experience for the customer. The engagement with the customer rarely ends with the purchase. In fact, the way the marketplace is designed promotes vendors to follow up with customers on each purchase, and to promptly fix any problems with it or risk having a bad review, which could be detrimental to future business. The app draws the user back often with games that the users can play to earn points and get discounts.

When the engagement with the customer extends beyond just the transaction, the brand's product and services become sticky, and the customer will tend to share its merits with more potential customers.

Treasure Every Bad Customer Situation

A bad experience for our customers is an excellent opportunity to show them just how much we truly care. And if all we can offer is an apology or a verbal commitment to not let this happen again, or even a waiver of charges for the transaction that was plagued by this bad experience, then we would have missed the chance to acquire a loyal customer.

Towards the end of the COVID-19 pandemic, restaurants started opening and were dangling special offers to lure customers back to a physical dining experience. So I decided to venture beyond my usual crop of eateries to visit this restaurant in a 5-star hotel in town. On my first visit there, I noticed that many of the diners seemed to know the staff there pretty well. They were having great conversations, everyone seemed happy and were smiling, and I wondered when it would be my turn to enjoy such rapport with the restaurant staff. Physical dining, in my opinion, is more than just eating and tasting the food. The people who attend to us as diners actually make a huge difference to the entire experience. On my second visit there, I noticed that the restaurant was fully booked and was short-handed. Naturally, service standards dropped drastically. Plus, I saw that some diners were not observing the safe distancing rules imposed by the government to slow the spread of COVID-19 and the restaurant staff didn't do anything about it. I tried to lodge a complaint to the staff on duty but things didn't seem to improve.

The entire experience wasn't as expected of a restaurant that charges a premium and held itself in high regard. Being a business owner myself, I felt the need to escalate this to the management instead of simply giving them a bad review on social media or TripAdvisor that would do more harm than good. So I wrote a lengthy email to whoever was the director in charge of this restaurant, detailing the entire experience and explaining why I thought that this was a serious matter that demanded remediation from his team. I also made it clear that I wouldn't want to escalate the matter further and ruin the recovery for the restaurant as life was already challenging because of the COVID-19 disruptions to dining out. In the email, I left my mobile number and made myself available for further clarifications, if needed.

The next day, the director for dining experience in the hotel called me. He apologised and agreed with my analysis. He promised to fix the problem with the operations team and he offered me a trip back to the restaurant for dinner to thank me for the feedback, and for giving them a chance to turn things around.

On my third visit, at the invitation of the director for dining experience, I was treated to one of the most delightful dining experiences I have had in a long time. Suffice to say that the restaurant pulled out all the stops to change my opinion of the way it conducts business.

Since then, I have become good friends with the staff in the restaurant, frequenting it every week and celebrating all special occasions there. Why? Simply because I realised that the staff and leadership there really sought to give me a great dining experience every time I stepped in. And they have not failed me since. In fact, I fell in love with the service standards so much that I couldn't stop telling my friends about the place, and would host business dinners there, and did I mention writing glorious reviews for them on Tripadvisor and Google?

Sometimes, when things screw up and our customers are affected, they don't really want to hear an apology and a promise that such things will not happen again – the customer would just like to be loved. How we do our customer recovery will determine if we can win a loyal customer who will tell his friends about us.

If we know what our customers want, then we would know what to do to make up for a bad experience. But if we only focus on what they need, then we would have most certainly missed the point. Our staff need to know how much we love our customers and how far we would go to win them back when hiccups happen. Our customer-facing team needs to be empowered to take remedial action on the fly, guided by a clear framework, so that our customers do not feel short-changed whenever a service standard has lapsed. For example, in Taobao, merchants are known to have people on standby 24-7 to answer any questions or complaints by customers at any time of the day and be able to offer remedies to appease a dissatisfied customer.

When our customer recovery actions say "We will do everything to make it right for you and to ensure that you will want to return to us because you can feel how sincere we are in having you back," and we act on that as proof, then we can say we have loved our customers.

Armed with an ADO and a customer-centred attitude, it's time to go to market.

8

Going to Market

"No plan survives contact with the enemy" is a common military saying that is reconfigured from older sayings of Winston Churchill, Dwight Eisenhower and Helmuth von Moltke (1800–1891), who was a German field marshal. No matter the amount of time and resources we spend on planning an attack, the assumptions on which we base our battle plan can quickly be proven wrong the moment we meet the enemy (the "contact") for the first time. And then it is up to the clever leader to adapt and pivot when faced with such an emergency during battle.

So, does this mean we shouldn't bother to plan but just hit the field immediately?

Of course not!

Even as one should expect to face the unexpected, planning is still paramount, according to Churchill and Eisenhower, who said "Plans are of little importance, but planning is essential" and "Plans are worthless, but planning is everything", respectively.

Graham Kenny, in his article for the *Harvard Business Review*,[41] advocates that strategic plans are less important than the act of

---

41   Graham Kenny, "Strategic Plans Are Less Important than Strategic Planning" *Harvard Business Review* (21 June 2016) <https://hbr.org/2016/06/strategic-plans-are-less-important-than-strategic-planning>.

strategic planning. He recommends that organisational leaders should view strategic plans as guidance tools rather than strict playbooks that must be followed blindly and that leaders should be prepared to look for discrepancy in the field, adapt and pivot accordingly as the team executes the plan.

A new venture opening its doors to business is likened to an army going into battle. In this chapter, I discuss some of the guidance points for a go-to-market (GTM) strategy of a new venture that is about to hit the market for the first time.

Remember that our aim is to pick up revenue traction as soon as we can and to qualify for an exit event in 36 months. So, we are racing against time from the moment we start the venture.

These GTM guidance points are meant to help the founder think systematically about the key aspects of the business so that he or she wastes no time in reaching the customers, and to acquire and retain them with high efficiency and minimum burn.

Guidance #1: Get the MVP Up and Hit the Road Fast

The concept of a Minimum Viable Product (MVP) originated from the book *The Lean Startup*,[42] a methodology for developing and launching new products or businesses. The MVP is the version of a product with the minimum set of features that can be released to early adopters, in order to gather feedback and validate assumptions about the product. The idea is to test the product with real users as quickly as possible, and then use that feedback to improve and iterate on the product.

Fast Founders use MVPs to rapidly test if their products and services are solving problems that are big enough for their target customers, and to quickly determine which features are most important to their users. Quite often, an enterprise needs to burn cash to develop an MVP that is fit for the market. To mitigate excessive burn and to ensure we get to the market as soon as possible, we need to get the

---

42   Eric Ries, *The Lean Startup – How Today's Entrepreneurs Use Continuous Innovation to Create Radically Successful Businesses* (Crown Business, 2011)

machinery up and running as early as Day 1 of a new venture and we can do this by creatively structuring the deals with potential partners in the early stages of bootstrapping, as I have discussed in the previous chapters (Chapter 5 "Make Your Numbers Talk" and Chapter 6 "Bootstrapping – Beg, Borrow, Build, Deal").

But to test any product with early adopters, we need to get to the customers first, and find data on the customers' behaviour that may suggest if our product or service is on the right track. And we cannot do that without first knowing who our customers are.

Guidance #2: Reach the Customer Quickly

New ventures and startups whose brands are not yet known in the market often struggle with getting to the market soon enough to get to a positive cash flow position and be profitable enough for investors to put in money to help it grow. The instinctive reaction of many founders I speak to is to jump onto digital marketing, doing Search Engine Optimisation (SEO), getting influencers to profile their products or paying their way through ads on different content and social media platforms. Those with a little more money to burn would engage a digital marketing agency to do the work. Unless the product is so awesome and it delivers an audaciously desirable experience to the user, these are "slow burn" activities that will deliver the sales eventually, but not in the short term. And if they do deliver sales, the cost of acquiring each paying customer would be exorbitant.

If we wish to build a new venture and qualify it for an exit in 36 months, we need to reach our target customers quickly, even as we bootstrap our operations, and then get them to start buying from us (the conversion), to keep using our products (the retention) and to tell their friends about us (the promotion). To achieve this outcome at rocket speed and with very little budget, we need to be wise to prioritise strategies that will work for us quickly against those that can help us build lasting impressions over the long term.

Let's explore the merits and relevance of some of these strategies that can help us to reach our target customers.

SEO Takes 18 Months to Show Results

SEO is the process of improving the visibility and ranking of a website or a web page in search engine results pages (SERPs). The goal of SEO is to increase the quantity and quality of traffic to a website through organic (non-paid) search results. The techniques in SEO include keyword research, content optimisation and backlink building – pretty technical stuff for someone not experienced in digital marketing. SEO efforts could take at least 18 months of continuous investment of at least US$3,500 per month before reasonable traction builds up. And that is if you have someone on your team who is an SEO expert or is working with an expert SEO consultant to do the job. Thus, if the intent is to launch fast, get the data to tweak, pivot or terminate the product line, we may not want to invest in this as the main strategy.

Influencers Build Brand Awareness, not Sales

An influencer is a person who has the ability to influence the purchasing decisions of others because of their authority, knowledge, position, or relationship with their audience. Influencers, also known as Key Opinion Leaders (KOLs), are often active on social media platforms and have a large following of people who are interested in the topics or products that they promote. Because of this ability, businesses engage influencers to promote their products or services to a wider audience. They do this by creating sponsored posts or videos that feature the product or service, or by hosting giveaways or contests in which their followers can enter to win the product or service.

Influencer marketing helps a brand to create a sense of authenticity that is not always possible with traditional forms of advertising. It can help bring in some traction and generate some useful information on product-to-market fit, and possibly good traction if the product is audaciously desirable for the target market. But I would consider it best deployed for brand building over the medium to long term.

So, if these methods are not necessarily effective in bringing in revenue in the short term without incurring super high burn multiples, what are some of the more affordable ways to get to the customer and get them to buy from us?

Get on the News as Often as You Can

While many may argue that the mainstream news media is no longer relevant given the advent of social journalism through platforms such as TikTok (or Douyin in China) and Instagram, I would argue that mainstream news media that have gained a steady following still command the respect of viewers who value credible journalism. These are not just the newspapers or TV broadcast stations that I am talking about. News channels these days take many forms and mostly exist on the cloud. They are also starting to take a range of hybrid forms that merge content produced by professional journalists and ordinary citizens to provide a comprehensive coverage of contemporary and current matters.

For example:

- 今日头条 in China (*Jīnrì tóutiáo*) is a very popular Chinese news and information platform that uses professional journalists and citizen journalists to gather and produce content for its subscribers. It also aggregates a wide variety of content, including news articles from professional news outlets, videos, images, and social media posts and works from independent bloggers, making it relevant to an incredibly diverse range of readers.
- In Indonesia, a highly popular news and content discovery app called "BaBeIndonesia" provides Indonesian language news for its subscribers. The platform curates breaking news and articles, videos and social media posts, and shares them with users based on their interests and behaviour.

The idea is to make the news as often as we can, to quickly become a thought leader in the subject matter and to inspire others to emulate us.

Making our clients famous drew attention to us

I have mentioned that in my second venture, I provided life sciences learning enrichment services to public schools, and after a brief stint of six months or so, our sales skyrocketed and we generated year-on-year revenue growth of more than 20x in 24 months from the start of operations.

The product we offered then was certainly an ADO to get that sort of traction. But remember that when we first offered it to our prospective clients, most felt that it was too audacious to be feasible and didn't believe that it could be done, nor thought that it was necessary for their students.

So how did we get to the point where most of our target clients wanted our services, and how did we get there fast enough since doing it organically by going door-to-door would have taken too long?

We made sure that our work with our client schools was well-known to the public.

I had a clear business goal: I wanted to make as many of my clients famous as possible.

I figured that since we were in the leading edge of science education, pioneering a way of teaching young students about highly sophisticated technologies, then the work of our clients could be the model for other schools to emulate. Each school that collaborated with me would be an example of innovation in education and details of such endeavours would be of interest to the public. And the press would be the ideal platform to get this information out there.

And we did all this without hiring a public relations (PR) firm. Our "PR team", comprising an intern, myself and one other colleague, collaborated with our clients to draft all the press releases for our clients to send out to the press. The school leaders whom we worked with all agreed that if the work was bringing in good outcomes in their students' learning and interests in STEM or science, then we should let the world know and they were very happy to explain to interested parties about our collaboration.

As a company, our target was to get one feature article in the news at least once every two months. And each time a news article or news feature came out, we would announce to the market our work with that client. This continuously put us in the leading edge of the industry, making us the undisputed thought leader in this domain. To do this, we needed to offer an innovative angle to learning about life sciences in school, constantly pushing the envelope and developing novel and newsworthy narratives for each school to work with. And this kept going for two years.

During this period, we didn't need to do much marketing as our phones kept ringing and because of the good work we did, our clients recommended us to their colleagues, further corroborating the narrative that we were excellent partners in education.

Here are some ways to get into the news:

- Find a novel angle for your work and frame the narrative as useful information for the public or specific groups in the market to know. The key is to ensure that knowing about your work is useful to the reader – something he or she could learn from, emulate or be inspired by. No news media outlet will be keen to cover features of your product or your company. But they may be open to talking about the impact it has on your clients, or even better, how your clients have impacted others, in part by using your product or service.
- Share a statistic you have gathered about the community that is of interest to the public. Statistical data and research reports are powerful tools to tell others that you know more than them, that you have access to information and insights on their lives that

they may not know.

- Give to and share generously with to those who cannot afford it but need your service. Remember that a good business should impact the world as we earn from it.

- Inspire, inspire, inspire. Dig deep within the organisation and see if there is something you do, someone you work with, something you've learned and practised, that inspires others to review, reflect and make changes to the way they live their lives.

Find Channel Partners to Help You Sell

Many companies make it their business to sell other people's products. These companies may have established excellent relationships with buyers in the ecosystem and if they agree to work with us to help sell or distribute our products, then it could be a cheap way to reach out to our customers. But it isn't that straightforward when seeking a distributor to sell for us. Getting a distributor to agree to invest resources to market and sell our products is a big ask and when the products don't sell well, we have no clarity on the real reasons behind the lack of performance – we may not have enough datapoints or touchpoints with the end user to know exactly what the real problem is, whether it's a lack in product-market fit because the product design doesn't solve a big enough problem for the customer or a case of the distributor not investing enough to get the product out there. A distributor who is performing relatively well may also demand a higher share of the revenue, and the cut to the distributor could be anything from 50 per cent to as much as 80 per cent, depending on the leverage of the distributor in a particular relationship. Thus, with all things considered, we need to be prudent when choosing to work with distributors or channel partners to resell our products. There are no rules as to whether a company should work with a distributor, but I would venture to suggest that we can consider working with a distributor if:

- Our venture is in its starting phases, when we are cash strapped and every dollar counts in getting to the market in as short a time as possible;
- We are venturing into a new market and we want to test if our solutions would resonate with the target audience there;
- Getting large groups of users with the intent of converting them to adopt a more comprehensive product is our main aim, and such a distribution partner can help get these users on board; or
- There are real and significant barriers to entering a new market, for example, cultural and language barriers that require the distributor to leverage its relationships in the market and possibly invest in product modifications.

Other types of channel partners may not simply resell our products to their customers but may licence selected components to be integrated into their core product. These structures are more complicated as it involves discussions on the granular aspects of intellectual property and the licensing mechanisms in the deal. But these deals could be worth a lot, sometimes involving millions of dollars in upfront licensing fees with royalties going forward.

Push on the Ground May Work in the Short Term

Several years ago, I was part of a delegation of tech entrepreneurs led by the government to visit some of the more successful tech startups in China. There we learned from one of the co-founders of a highly successful travel app startup that in their early stages, in order to get users to experience their app, they did *di-tui* (地推), which literally translates to "push-on-the-ground". It involves positioning people in crowded spaces like the train stations and shopping malls to distribute flyers with QR codes on them to get people to download the app, and then dangling lots of promotions to get them to use the app to make their first travel booking. It got this startup a large group of users, who after using the app, fell in love with it and the number of users just kept growing. This method still works today.

Another iteration of this strategy is to set up temporary experience centres in places where our target customers would gather. This allows them to experience using our product while our staff explain to them how much more awesome this product is and how they can use it in different ways. Experience centres are one of those places where we can land our first sale from a visiting customer. But for this to work, the experience shouldn't be a fleeting one, like tasting a sample of food from a booth in a busy supermarket, as a brief sensory experience may not be enough to tip a prospect over and land a sale. At experience centres, we need to convince prospective customers to stick around long enough to experience the product or service we provide, while we pitch it to them subtly to help them decide that they need it, in order to get them to sign up on the spot.

Guidance #3: Convert, Retain and Promote

Having reached the target customers and getting them to use our products, we need to find a way to monetise these users. For tech-based ventures, there are many ways to monetise the users of their products and many companies have applied creative methods to make money out of their users, with the most common being having free users converting to paid ones in a freemium model.

Having converted a user into a paying customer is just the start. There is no point in being able to get lots of customers to buy from us if they do not stick around or return to buy more. There is a name to describe this phenomenon, where a customer signs on a subscription programme with us and terminates the subscription after some time. It is called "churn". The extent to which churn happens over a fixed period (such as each month) is called the churn rate. Churn rate is expressed as a percentage of those who "drop off" over the customers we have at the beginning of that period:

$$\textbf{Churn rate} = \frac{\text{Number of Customers that cancelled the subscription at the end of the period}}{\text{Number of Customers we signed on at the beginning of the same period}}$$

For example, if a company starts with 100 customers and loses 20 of them over the course of a month, the churn rate for that month would be 20 per cent.

The churn rate is an important metric when tracking the performance of businesses with recurring revenue, such as subscription-based services, software-as-a-service (SaaS) and telecommunications. The higher the churn rate, the more a company will need to invest to get new customers on board to maintain or grow its revenue. Thus, if all we have are lots of one-time purchases from our customers, and if each purchase ticket isn't high, then we may end up losing money in the end, because the cost to get a customer to make that purchase may be higher than the revenue we get from that sale, especially if we have spent a lot of money on advertising.

Let's explore this further as we dive deeper into using paid advertising to get conversions.

Pay Attention to CAC

Paid advertising costs on social media platforms and blogs contribute to the total Customer Acquisition Cost (CAC). CAC is an important component of the business as it directly affects how much the enterprise will need to spend to get one customer to buy a unit of product. When we compare this figure against the Lifetime Value of the customer (LTV), we can derive if our business is profitable on its own.

CAC can range from $50 to $250 to as high as $3,000 per customer. This is because advertising and lead generation is only one component of the process, and that alone could cost more than a few hundred dollars per lead. To get a customer on board and pay for our services, we need to invest in a sales team to close the sale. And depending on the nature of the services we provide, we may also need to offer a trial experience for the customer, just like offering a sample product to a new customer.

As mentioned in our discussion on gross margins, in some industries such as the online tutoring industry, the CAC can be up to $3,000 per student who signs up for a $1,000 course. In such instances, the business will need to ensure that it retains this same customer for two more repeated purchases before it breaks even.

Now here is where it can get tricky: if we need this same customer to repeat a purchase for at least two more times before we break even, and each purchase may last for, say, ten weeks, then what is the likelihood that our competitors may offer this same customer a better deal after her first ten weeks of subscription with us, possibly at a lower prices and comparable quality with a few more perks thrown in? In the highly competitive tutoring industry, this is more likely to happen than not, as each player vies for more market share, at which point, we need to ask, "How long will this last before we see a turnaround towards profitability?"

There are important questions to consider when looking at the CAC for our offering. For example:

- Is the CAC higher than the LTV of a customer? If so, what is our plan to lower the CAC or increase the LTV such that the CAC becomes substantially lower than LTV in order for the business to be profitable?
- Is our churn rate too high for us to make money, given our CAC? If so, how do we make our offering more sticky for the customer?
- How effective are our paid advertising campaigns? Are there ways to reduce CAC by channelling the paid advertising budget to other means that could result in higher conversion rates?

To answer these questions, we need to understand a little more about what the customer needs to be convinced to buy something, and how to get that to him or her in our go-to-market process.

Customers Need Corroborating Evidence to Buy-In

In discussing how to change anyone's mind, Jonah Berger[43] described customers' need for proof in order to reach a buying decision. The amount, source and frequency of the evidence depends largely on the knowledge of the brand and the price of the product. Generally, the greater the brand awareness, the lower the amount of evidence is needed to convince the buyer to purchase. Cost-wise, the higher the cost of the product or service, the greater the amount of evidence is needed to trigger a purchase by a customer.

The author observed that when such evidence comes from a variety of sources and from people we see to be similar to us, we are more likely to trust the evidence. When this is coupled with more successive appearance versus spacing the evidence between a long period of time, the momentum builds up towards a buying decision. Thus, if the corroborating evidence is provided by the supplier of the product instead of its users, and the time between such proofs is far apart (for example, two months apart), then it is likely that the effect of that corroborative evidence will not be strong enough to trigger a buying decision in the customers who see it.

Corroborating evidence can come in many forms, such as news coverage, a review by an influencer or even paid advertising. I have discussed the merits of these ways in the previous section and we now know that not all methods work well in the short term. One type of corroborating evidence that we find highly effective is in the form of social e-commerce recommendations.

Social E-Commerce or Social Selling

Corroborating evidence is most credible when it comes from people you trust. And that's the power of social selling by micro influencers.

43   Jonah Berger, *The Catalyst – How to Change Anyone's Mind* (Simon & Schuster, 2020).

Micro influencers are individuals who use the products they review. They are also called Key Opinion Consumers (KOCs). Their following is generally much smaller than mainstream influencers (KOLs) but they have more intimate interactions with their followers since these followers share the same interests as them and are likely their friends and extended family members. There is thus a greater sense of trust in what they say.

There are platforms that can help us to access a potentially large number of KOCs that may want to try out our products, while other platforms can get interested KOCs to be our affiliates and sell our products to their network of followers. However, getting KOCs on board to try out our product may not mean much until they agree to sell it for us, as can be seen in the example below.

In the midst of COVID-19, HomeExplorer, an education company in China, decided to launch a home-based multisensory experience kit for parents to let their children be exposed to world class learning from a box that is delivered to the subscriber every two weeks. To launch the product and test its relevance in China, the company collaborated with a social platform in China that curates new products for a selected group of micro influencers to register for the opportunity to test-drive and publish their reviews on the platform. When the platform opened the registration to its micro influencers, many came forth to put up their interest to test and review the product. In fact, the number of registrants was so large that the product ranked in the top five most popular pilot products in that campaign. For a small company with an unknown brand, this was huge as it suggested that the concept of the product was appealing to the target customers.

Two weeks after the sample boxes were sent to selected KOCs to try out, more than 90 per cent of the micro influencers posted their video reviews and amongst those reviews, less than five per cent were negative reviews. Again, it suggested that the product might have something going for it in the target market. The team was elated.

From this point, it all went downhill. When the company sought to collaborate with these micro influencers to help promote the product to their followers, no one stepped forward to sign on as an affiliate. None of the micro influencers who gave good reviews thought the product was good enough for them to sell to their network. So, this product line did not meet the mark for those KOCs. In the end, HomeExplorer had to discontinue the campaign and decided to pull the product from the market.

As we can see from this example, HomeExplorer's home-centric education product probably wasn't able to solve a problem for parents, at least not to the point that would make them recommend it to their friends. As the product wasn't audaciously desirable to the target customers, it didn't gain traction.

But this is not the end of the story for this product because it did succeed in the end, but in another market, for another group of customers. I will discuss how this happened in the section "Guidance #4: Know Your Market".

When we manage to get KOCs to sell for us, the sales can be quite phenomenal and for an unknown brand from a small company, it may be all that we need to prove the value of our solution and justify investing further to take it to the next level. Best of all, we get to see the results fast. In the words of a digital marketing expert who operates a social e-commerce platform, on which one micro influencer managed to sell close to 1,000 bottles of an unknown brand of shampoo, "Even if your product doesn't sell well through social e-commerce, you will at least have the data to know what the problem is, and to decide if you want to iterate it further or shut it down."

Build a Small Army to Close B2B Sales

Sometime towards the end of 2022, I had an insightful discussion with the founder and CEO of one of the region's most successful digital marketing services companies, with operations in Singapore, Malaysia and Vietnam. His clients included some of the biggest consumer brands and online marketplaces. Working with these big brands has already gotten his hands full. The digital marketing service business is good. Yet, he lamented that in his latest fundraising exercise, the valuation of the company seems pretty modest, based on a formula of a small price-to-earnings (P/E) multiple. He told me that the investors and even his broker did not understand his business. So, I asked him to walk me through his business to be sure I understood it.

At the end of his presentation, I discovered that this company had a gem in its backyard that no one seemed to notice, including him as the founder – it owns and operates an online database of more than five million micro influencers who were ready to take on jobs with companies big and small, on an average fee chargeable to the client ranging from $5,000 to $10,000 per assignment. That's not all. Each day, more than 50 small and medium businesses would visit the micro influencer platform, and the data suggested that these businesses were warm leads or sales qualified leads (SQLs), ready to buy a service from the company. Yet, the company hadn't monetised these SQLs. The reason? He felt that monetising this group of smaller clients was a high touch process, requiring a separate team of sales staff to close these sales. He concluded that it wasn't worth the effort and resources to develop this part of the business.

I was baffled. I worked through the numbers with the founder and the unit economics of hiring 20 staff to close these warm leads and before I could finish calculating, he exclaimed, "Oh, it means that if I could close even 15 per cent of these leads, my revenue would increase substantially each month!"

Errr, yeah … how is it that you've only realised it now?

Sometimes, in B2B sales, we need to look hard at the data on hand. If we have access to a certain group of customers who can be brought on board without much investment in the first place, then we could be sitting on a mountain of gold, and we need to get a team to dig deep and harvest. But do the maths carefully first. Be sure that the economics checks out and always test if these leads are really ready to take on our services. Then once this hypothesis is proven to be true, be bold and invest to harvest quickly.

Track your Net Promoter Score and Churn Rate Religiously

I met with an entrepreneur who told me that she's confident that her startup can grow rapidly as she has designed the product in such a way that current users will get more users on board and before long, there will be an exponential growth of paid users. I was curious and asked her how she knows that this will happen? More importantly, what data does she have to convince me that this can happen? It turned out that she didn't have any data to suggest this, although she did have information that would suggest that her current users would be very disappointed if she were to go out of business.

"That's really good. But this data merely suggests that your product is sticky. It doesn't suggest that it is awesome enough for them to tell others about it."

This startup has a low churn rate, but an unknown Net Promoter Score.

The Net Promoter Score (NPS) measures the likelihood that a customer would tell another customer about our offering, promoting it to new customers. It indicates whether the offering is appealing enough to spread by word of mouth, which drastically reduces the CAC for the company. The score ranges from 1 to 10 and is normally obtained through surveys or conversations with customers, and tabulating the average of all individual scores. Any score lower than 8.5 would suggest that the offering has yet to reach a point of self-promotion and the company would need to spend more effort to maintain the momentum of acquiring new customers.

Extending my earlier discussion on churn rate, a high churn rate suggests that our products and services are not sticky enough for the customer to continue using it and it is a cause for concern.

Companies with low churn rates and low NPS would suggest that while the product may be sticky enough, it isn't awesome enough to be audaciously desirable. And so the customers don't feel driven to talk about it to their friends. To grow the customer base, these companies will need to keep investing to get new customers on board in a linear fashion (the more we invest, the more customers we get).

Contrast that with a product that has low churn rates and high NPS. It suggests that the company may be at an inflection point on a trajectory of rapid growth and a little push from external investors may just do the trick.

High **Churn Rate**	Serious problem with product-market-fit. Consider drastic redesign or pivot.	Product sales likely a one-time purchase model with few repeated purchases. Product is awesome enough for its owners to tell others about it.
Low	Product is sticky, but not awesome enough to spread by word of mouth. Constant push needed to bring in new customers.	Product is sticky and awesome enough for users to promote to others. Product user growth at an inflection point, heading towards exponential growth.
	Low	High

Net Promoter Score

We need to constantly track NPS, churn rates and CAC to help us get a good picture of how our customers are behaving towards what we are offering, then combine this analysis with regular conversations with our customers to get insights on how to tweak our MVP to be an ADO.

Guidance #4: Know Your Market

A Business that Thrives in One Territory doesn't Mean it Will Thrive in Another

Back to my business in life sciences enrichment education for schools in Singapore, which got so much media attention and gained so much traction that the venture went from a company of one to more than 30 full-time staff and more than 70 part-time staff within a year. As mentioned earlier, our work was plastered in all the mainstream news media in Singapore. Despite getting an acquisition offer in the second year of the business (more of that in Chapter 10 "The Exit – Sell, Float or Close"), we have always thought that the Singapore market is too small to make this business interesting enough to excite investors. So we aggressively expanded into the region, on the same model as our Singapore business. We raised money from investors who were based in Singapore as well as those based in the respective countries. Those weren't naive investors – they were venture capitalists, family offices and successful entrepreneurs themselves who saw the potential for the same service in their countries. Three years later, we decided to close them all down.

So, what happened?

I learned a painful lesson in this loop around Asia and back, that just because something has worked in Singapore, we should never assume that it would work elsewhere, and this is especially true for the education business targeting public schools. Our model worked beautifully in Singapore because the Ministry of Education was determined to enrich the education of its students and provided generous grants to students in Singapore to pay for enrichment services like the type we offered in our core business. That support mechanism did not exist elsewhere. So for every dollar we spent acquiring one customer in Singapore, we needed to spend ten times more to do so in a regional country. Plus, such premium learning experiences were only accessible to a few schools in each major city, not to mention the lack of skilled teachers whom we could employ in those countries to deliver the lessons. All these disrupted the unit economics of our business and, in the end, it didn't seem worthwhile to continue, so we ended it.

Interestingly, 15 years later, I was given an opportunity to invest in an education company in China which was doing very similar things to what we had done. This company was gaining traction and looked promising. This was 15 years after I had started doing the same thing in Singapore.

So, when expanding regionally, timing, support mechanisms and access to skilled labour that is inherent in each society will determine the share of market. It is crucial to be prudent when expanding one's business after having a great run in the home market. We need to choose our target market carefully, then test out our solutions there quickly to validate our offering and to evaluate if it qualifies as an ADO there before investing further. Being ahead of time doesn't always pay.

A Failed Product in a B2C Market May Work Well in a B2B Market in Another Place

Let's return to HomeExplorer's education product that failed in China despite initial strong positive feedback from micro influencers' tests and reviews on social media. This same product actually proved to be a roaring success in another territory in Central Asia.

The difference: in China, the target market was parents (B2C) and the target solution was for home use; in Central Asia, the target market was teachers and the Ministry of Education (B2B) in that country, for use in schools, to level-up the students en masse through world class education products.

The same product targeting a different market somewhere else could become a hit. It so happened that the Ministry of Education in that Central Asian country was looking for an end-to-end solution, complete with learning resources, guides for teachers and equipment for use by students, and this product checked all the boxes beautifully. Of course, there were many details, nuts and bolts along the way that needed to be sorted and ironed out, but in the end, the company won a major contract to supply the product to tens and thousands of students that year.

	China	Central Asia
Target Customer	Parents	Ministry of Education
Target User	Children at home	Teachers in schools
Nature	B2C/D2C	B2B
Core Desired Interest	Engaged & fun learning	Nationwide upskilling for children
Core design product attributes demanded by customer	Rich repertoire, fun to use, design engaging to children on its own.	Domain thought leadership, teacher playbook.

Up to this point, I have discussed the paradigm a fast founder should have and the types of elements in a plan for executing a go-to-market strategy at high speed.

In the next two chapters, I will discuss matters concerning shoring up financial resources by fundraising and exiting a business at the right time.

9

Raising Money for the First Time

"Do you know how much capital in private equity is floating around out there, waiting to be deployed?" a senior executive at one of the world's largest sovereign wealth funds asked me.

"$200 billion? … $500 billion?"

$1 trillion. That was how much money that funds had and needed to deploy as investments into companies. "That's why my friends in private equity are all becoming billionaires!" he laughed, as he tried to help me understand just how much money there was out there and how companies with investment calls of smaller ticket sizes may never get the attention of the big funds.

That was in early 2022.

All that changed towards the end of that same year.

"It's very challenging to raise funds these days," a fund manager said to me in November 2022. "Some other funds have only managed to close less than 30 per cent of their target," another told me in early 2023.

The seismic shifts in the capital markets as we turned the corner of 2022 into 2023 have changed the perspective of many investors on how they see an investable asset. While there is still sizable interest in companies that are registering high growth in lieu of profitability, that interest is quickly waning. Companies that used to command high valuations despite losing money have to settle for "down rounds", with new money invested into them at drastically lower valuations. Those with cash are holding off from raising money for the next 24 to 36 months, in the hope that the "funding winter" will be over soon.

"Growth at all cost" gave way to "Clear path towards profitability", and is increasingly evolving towards just "Profitable companies with good growth potential."

There are several reasons that have led to this rapid change in the investment climate: drastic increase in interest rates, crazy inflation, the war in Ukraine and crypto crashes are just a few of them. The focus of this chapter is not to explain how the world has come to this current state – curious readers can find many good reads online to assuage their interest.

I want to discuss something more pragmatic for the new venture founder: what do many investors look for in a worthy investment target in this climate, how can we prime our venture to get invested and, just as importantly, when to get invested.

To start off, it may be helpful to be acquainted with who these investors are and how they invest. I will also discuss a few paradigms concerning fundraising and investment thesis formulation that founders should be aware of when they prepare to go down this road.

Types of Investors

Financial investors can be broadly grouped into angel investors, family offices, venture capitalists, private equity funds, venture debt providers and corporate ventures. Generally, venture capitalists, private equity funds and venture debt investors are considered institutional investors which are organisations that manage investment funds on behalf of their clients, with the goal of generating returns and preserving capital for their clients. Institutional investors often do this through systematic, research-driven methods to arrive at investment decisions.

Let's delve deeper into the characteristics of each investor group and the role it can play in a new venture that is looking to raise capital.

Angel Investors are high net worth individuals who can be entrepreneurs, senior executives or people who have inherited a big chest of money. These individuals tend to scrutinise the business a lot less than the other investors and tend to write investment cheques faster with less aggressive terms. They may also not request for a seat on the board. The limitation to raising funds from this group is that the cheque sizes tend to be small, typically ranging from $50,000 to $200,000 per ticket.

Family Offices (FOs) are more professionally managed money from high net worth individuals. Because FOs would typically employ professionals to source for and select deals for approval by the principal (the owner of the fund that is managed by the FO), the process may be more elaborate and thorough than that of angel investors. As part of the investment evaluation process, FOs may conduct some bits of due diligence, involving limited checking on the legal and financial matters of the company and the viability of the business. The good thing about raising from FOs is that the cheque sizes per FO may be bigger than from individual angel investors.

Generally, however, we shouldn't expect angel investors and FOs to help us much in strategic ways, such as helping us to grow our revenue or raising money from institutional investors in the later stages (there are exceptions, of course, and I have seen angel investors who have helped their invested companies access very strategic channel partners, but these are rare).

Venture Capitalists (VCs) may invest in early or late stage ventures, cutting cheque sizes of varying amounts. VCs have a relatively short runway and wouldn't prefer to stay on in the company for longer than a few years. However, they can be a good partner to have to prepare the company for subsequent rounds of investments.

Private Equity (PE) Investors tend to invest in later stage companies or mature companies that have a proven track record and a stable revenue stream. These investors used to prefer coming in at a stage when the company was growing rapidly or preparing for some form of exit in the foreseeable future. But these days, many have started moving upstream to earlier stage companies, as long as they see the growth potential in them. The investment cheque sizes from these investors are also not small, usually at least $10 million per ticket.

Corporate Ventures are the venture arms of large corporations and they typically invest in companies that have a strategic fit to their core business. With the right fit, a strategic corporate venture can help a company go far, by availing its resources, network and expertise. Their investment ticket size varies but they tend to demand a relatively substantial stake of 30 per cent and above in the company and some level of oversight in the company's operations. Some corporations invest in early stage companies with a view to acquire them eventually.

Not all investments involve a straightforward purchase of shares for cash. Sometimes, these investments are structured as convertible debt, where the loan provided by the investor is converted to shares of the company using a formula that everyone in the deal would agree on, usually based on the company's performance in the future.

A note of caution to founders when considering taking on a convertible debt as the instrument for an investment: if not structured well enough to protect the founders' interests in the company, a convertible debt, on conversion to shares, can result in the investor taking a substantial stake of the company and can even dilute a founder's share to a small percentage, and relinquishing the founder's control over the company. The founder needs to be cautious when negotiating such investments with any investor due to the possibility of losing the company if the debt is not structured properly or the founder has no leverage. More on that in my discussion on the dreaded down round when we need to raise capital to survive.

<u>Venture Debt</u> is a special class of debt instruments that is provided by specialised lenders, known as venture debt firms, and is typically used by early-stage or high-growth companies that may not yet be profitable or have significant assets to use as collateral. These investors adopt a similar level of stringency as VCs in evaluating the investee venture's potential to decide whether to lend money to the company. At first glance, debt doesn't seem attractive as taking on debt would add to the liabilities of the company. But debt may not be a bad thing as taking on debt instead of sacrificing shares in the company in the early stages can help the founders to preserve more shares for themselves. It is inevitable that their shares will be diluted down the road with subsequent rounds of fundraising, but the shares are probably the cheapest to an investor at the early stage of a venture. This means that any investor could own a sizable chunk of the company without putting in a lot of money, and this is not good for the founders as they could lose control of the company prematurely. Yet, there are inherent risks associated with taking on any kind of debt by a company. There is also the risk to founders that is associated with taking on debt, such as serving as personal guarantors to the loan (see the section "Fundraising Paradigm #5: Don't Celebrate", on fundraising related challenges facing founders).

Ultimately, the founder needs to embrace the possibility that any good rapport with an investor can quickly deteriorate down the road if the relationship isn't managed well. Because of this, the founder should always be prudent in negotiating the deal with the investor, get professionals on board to advise or facilitate, talk to other founders to hear their experiences with raising money from the same investor, and be prepared to walk away and find someone else if you're not comfortable with the investing party or the way the deal is structured.

Who Should We Pick?

"We want to bring in investors who can help us grow," is a common position of new ventures or startup founders. But are we clear on the sort of help we hope to get from investors, other than the funds they provide? And are these investors able to offer this kind of non-monetary help? A lot depends on the stage of the company and the sort of help that founders hope to get from them. But since this book is written for the new venture founder, I have limited the discussion to the typical needs of new ventures.

The help we need	The type(s) of investors we could partner	How they can help
Reach to other partners who can help increase our revenue.	Angel Investors	They may have invested or even owned companies that could be a potential customer for us, so they see the fit with our enterprise as we solve a problem that they may be facing.
	Early Stage VCs	They may have a portfolio that is focused on the industry where we operate, and have an ecosystem of companies that we can tap on for collaboration.

The help we need	The type(s) of investors we could partner	How they can help
Funds to start things off quickly without getting expensive lawyers in the mix to negotiate the deal.	Angel Investors	They provide the money quickly enough.
	Early Stage VCs	These investors have money to put into companies that interest them without much negotiations needed. VCs may require more engagement with the founders and their team.
More hands-on involvement and oversight to guide the enterprise while providing leads and help to increase revenue and scale operations.	Corporate/Strategic Investors	They are likely a potential customer and see a fit of what we do and what they need. They could have access to a wider customer base that we can tap on.

The journey to raise money can be likened to dating. There's the "getting to know you" phase, and the "liking-you-enough to go on more dates" phase, before the "let's get married" phase. At the liking-you-enough phase, the investor and the target are beginning to see a "meeting of minds and hearts" as both parties move towards getting "married" (the signing of an investment deal).

If an investor really likes us, we can sometimes hear offers of non-monetary help, such as:

- "We have the resources to help you scale";
- "You can tap on our [attributes and resources, network, etc] to grow your business";
- "We want you to succeed so we will want to help you along the way"; or
- "You fit very well within our [ecosystem, core business]".

This would be great, and such offers can often be genuine. But as a new venture, we need to be sure that we can indeed access such help, so we should try to tap on the offered resources first before jumping into signing any investment contract with the investors. For example, if the investor says he has the network to help us succeed, test this out first by asking to meet one of the companies in the network to see if you can sell anything to that company; if an investor says he owns an ecosystem of companies that could be our client, then ask him to instruct one of the companies to buy from you to be sure.

Startup founders may find this counterintuitive, since the whole idea of fundraising is to get the money in the first place. Because these offers are often accompanied by more stringent requirements and onerous conditions in the investment deal – ranging from what you can or cannot do as a founder after they put in the money, to how many board seats and/or how much oversight they want in the running of the company – the founder needs to be prudent at the outset and be prepared to walk away from the deal if the "help" does not commensurate with the loss of "freedom" going forward.

We should never raise money when we are desperate. The less desperate we are for fresh funds, the better position we are in to negotiate a good deal for ourselves. More on that later in this chapter, as I discuss the paradigms founders should have when raising money.

The Process

Generally, the process of raising money for the first time comprises more or less the following sequence:

- Step 1: sending the teaser investment deck of the company to the prospective investor.
- Step 2: pitching to the investor in person.
- Step 3: meeting the investor again, likely in the company's premises to introduce the team.
- Step 4: clarifying questions from the investor concerning

anything, from the contracts on hand to the opportunity ahead, and everything in between.

- Step 5: investor shows interest to invest and issues a non-binding term sheet, detailing the broad terms of the investment (for example, amount to invest, the financial instrument to be used, the valuation of the company prior to or after the money has been invested, etc).
- Step 6: due diligence (DD) begins, mainly of legal due diligence (LDD) and financial due diligence (FDD), where the investor may hire two groups of professionals to audit the legal contracts and the financials of the company.
- Step 7: (assuming that the DDs are cleared) preparation of the subscription and shareholders agreements.
- Step 8: signing of agreements and transfer of funds.
- Step 9: fulfilling any conditions that are precedent to the investment within a time frame after the money is received.

This process could take up to four months for an early stage venture that is less than two years old and could take substantially longer for older companies whose accounts are not audited in the years leading up to the fundraising exercise.

Depending on the type of investors we seek out in this early stage, the process may vary from this sequence. For example, angel investors are less likely to call for a detailed DD process while corporate investors, PE funds or investment of quantums that are larger than $10 million are likely to have an extensive DD process that could stretch for months.

So, before a founder jumps in for the first time to raise capital for his or her new venture, I would recommend a few paradigms to have in mind when thinking about when to fundraise, why fundraise, when to avoid a fundraise. It is important to get into the process with our eyes open, and be able to embrace any consequences that may come with an investment from a third party.

Fundraising Paradigm #1: Raise Money When You Don't Need It

Jack Ma, the founder of Alibaba, once said that companies should raise money when they don't need it because it gives them more leverage and flexibility in the future. And he is not alone in thinking this way.

This is because any investor who puts money into a company is doing so with the intention to make more money in the foreseeable future. So, if there are good reasons to suggest that this company won't make money for the investor, or worse, that this company could run the risk of getting into financial trouble, or even worse, that the investment target has a high risk of going bankrupt, then a sensible investor would pull back from committing the funds to that venture.

But when a company raises money that it doesn't have an immediate need for, it accumulates resources that enables it to capture new opportunities, to invest in growth and expansion. Plus, doing so will put it in a stronger position to negotiate with investors for much friendlier terms than when it seems desperate for a cash injection.

Fundraising Paradigm #2: People Invest to Grow a Company, Not Sustain it

No one likes to throw good money into a bad business. And if the business does not look like it can sustain itself without the investment, it risks not being able to convince investors in its fundraising round. Even in the current economic climate and funding winter, there is still a fair bit of dry powder or money for investment out there to be committed to promising targets. But these days, investors are spoilt for choice on which targets to put money in.

What may be different now is that investors would rather put more money into fewer good projects than to put a little into many just to see which ones may emerge as promising ones later on.

And investors are more likely to consider a company that is already self-sustaining than one that needs new money to survive. In other

words, founders should be raising money to grow the business and
not to sustain it.

Self-sustaining companies have these characteristics:

1. **Positive cash flow on a monthly basis**

   This means they collect more money (cash inflow) than they
   spend (cash outflow). These companies are able to sustain their
   ongoing operations with their current business activities. Cash
   inflow can take different forms, from actual receipts of cash from
   customers in a store to advance payments for work not yet done,
   periodic subscription payments made at the beginning of the
   subscription period or even loans from banks, to name a few.

2. **A strong and growing pipeline**

   A B2B company that shows promise would have signed on
   customers in its order books. This committed pipeline of
   customers or projects gives clear indication of the estimated
   amount of revenue the company is expected to generate and by
   when in the course of the year. A growing pipeline, however,
   will show a list of prospective customers that the company will
   sign on in the foreseeable future. Having a strong committed
   pipeline proves that the company's products and services are real
   and customers are prepared to pay for them. Having a growing
   pipeline will suggest to investors that what's currently in the
   order books could only be the start of the growth trajectory and
   that the company is likely going to grow a lot more, giving the
   investors confidence that the money invested will generate more
   in the future.

3 **Ability to withstand the DD drag**

   DD is a process that investors undertake to audit a company's
   business in depth before deciding on whether to invest in it. It
   usually involves specialist auditors and lawyers that are engaged
   by the investor to go through all the legal agreements and
   financial operations of the company, verifying them to be true to

what the company claims to be when pitching for the investment. It could take anything from a few weeks to a few months, depending on the size of the investment, the age of the company and whether the company's records are intact and audited yearly.

In an investors' market, where there is an abundance of investment opportunities available and investors have a strong bargaining position, investors have the liberty to study the company closely, delve deeper into the operations of the company, look closely at its cashflow position, order books, realisable receivables, all legal agreements and so on, before deciding whether to invest or not. All these means that the DD process just gets longer. In fact, I may even argue that some investors may be tempted to drag the DD process to see if the enterprise does have enough to be sustainable in the first place. This bodes well for the one with the cash to invest, since they can take a longer time to get to know the founders and their nuances, while "testing" to see if the company can sustain itself without help as a form of risk assessment of the target. Nothing wrong with this posture and nothing "cold" or "heartless" about being clinical in assessing if the target has what it takes to be investment-worthy.

Depending on the type of investor and the investment ticket size, founders of companies more than two years old should be prepared to comfortably walk this DD process for at least six to 18 months, maybe even longer, while founders of startups should be prepared for a four to six-month journey.

4. <u>Already profitable</u>

It doesn't matter if the company is a startup or a mature company that has been around for several years, these days, investors are more attracted to companies that make money at the end of each quarter or year as it suggests that the risks associated with this investment is mitigated relative to other companies that are not profitable and are still burning cash on a quarterly basis.

If my company is already so stable financially, why do I even need to raise money?

In my recent conversations with VCs to discuss the attributes of an investable venture, one VC manager remarked jokingly that if a venture already possesses these self-sustaining attributes, the founder is not likely to want his money. I can understand where this observation came from as I, too, used to feel this way when I was running one of my ventures that was "doing well".

Recall that investors put money in any new venture to make more money by helping the enterprise to grow faster. If the point of raising capital is to grow the enterprise, then we need to ask ourselves:

> If I am selling x number of units in one location, and making a profit of Y dollars per month, can I set up 10, 20 or 100 more locations and make 100x more revenue and possibly > 100Y profits per month? If so, do I have the money in the bank to do so? If not, can I raise capital to help me get there?

In Chapter 8 "Going to Market", I emphasised that speed is crucial to the initial success of a company. Ideally, a company should be so cash rich that it is able to invest in projects to capture new opportunities and scale on its own. But this is rarely the case, especially for new ventures. So, the company could do with a bit of help from investors who are aligned to its vision.

While investors may be attracted to companies that are self-sustainable, they are more likely to invest in those that have a strong case for growth. Because we are dealing with a new venture, it is unlikely that the venture is already experiencing explosive growth at the early stages of its development, and investors at this stage will be looking for signs that suggest the venture will grow at an unprecedented rate post-investment.

So, what does a company with a strong growth potential look like?

Fundraising Paradigm #3: Investors Look for Growth Potential Indicators

A financial or strategic investor will tend to seek answers to the following questions when assessing the growth potential of a new venture that is raising funds for the first time:

1. Does it operate in a big enough market?
2. Does it have a clear and promising growth narrative (the story)?
3. Is its positioning in the market distinctly blue ocean, with an ADO?
4. How high is the gross profit margin? Does it meet the Rule of 40?
5. Is it led by a strong enough team with complementary skills, network, experience and expertise to realise the growth narrative?
6. Who else is interested in investing?

I have addressed the matter of market sizing (Question 1), growth story (Question 2), market positioning (Question 3) and the team dynamics of the founders and their associates (Question 5) in the earlier chapters.

The "Rule of 40"[44]

In Chapter 5 "Make Your Numbers Talk", I have also discussed the relevance of EDITDA or profit margin analysis (Question 4). Let's build on this to discuss how this is relevant to the "Rule of 40" that institutional investors such as VCs and PE funds use to evaluate the potential of a startup. In the Rule of 40, the sum of a startup's growth rate and its profitability margin should be around 40 per cent or more.

> Rule of 40:
> Revenue Growth Rate + EDITDA Margin = 40%

---

44 Brad Feld, "The Rule of 40 For a Healthy SaaS Company" Archives (3 February 2015) <https://feld.com/archives/2015/02/rule-40-healthy-saas-company/>.

where the revenue growth can be calculated on a year-over-year (YOY), quarterly or even monthly basis.

The Rule of 40 is often used as a benchmark and a rule of thumb for a quick evaluation of the investment opportunity in a startup, especially if it is in the software-as-a-service or SaaS business. This is because such companies operate on really high profit margins. It needs to be noted that this rule doesn't apply to other industries but as a good practice, a founder should try to run his or her enterprise to meet this rule where possible.

If a startup scores above this benchmark, it is considered to be a strong investment opportunity. Conversely, scoring below this benchmark can be considered to be a weaker opportunity. But this is only a rule of thumb and investors will probably consider other important factors that I have discussed here and in the other chapters when evaluating a startup as a potential investment.

This leaves us with the last question: Who else has shown interest to invest in the new venture?

Find Someone Credible to Lead the Fundraising Round

Investors seldom like to be the first in on the deal, especially when the target is a new venture that is raising money for the first time. So where possible, we should try to find a credible investor to lead the way. This investor could be an angel investor who is well respected in the investment community, or an institutional investor. The lead investor does the first set of evaluations and may be prepared to undertake downstream activities such as the DD of the company prior to investment commitment. With a lead investor secured, it may be easier to attract other investors to come on board.

Fundraising Paradigm #4: Never Raise Capital to Survive

This is true especially for founders whose ventures have raised money in the past and now faces the predicament of the company running out of cash to sustain itself. These founders might have raised money some time back at a certain valuation, which is no longer valid. So, they can only interest investors if they significantly reduce the valuation of their enterprise in order to bring in much needed capital to sustain the business. In this situation, the founders will be raising money in a *down round*.

In down rounds, the investor typically calls the shots and if we are not careful, we could get an investment on terms that are so aggressive that the founder and some earlier angel investors may be wiped out in the deal – the founder may effectively lose control of the company.

In his article on how to survive in a down round,[45] Jon Medved cautioned that in a down round, an investor with deep pockets who sees the long-term fundamentals of the company could give money to the company at a time when it needs it most, presumably on predatory terms and effectively wipe out the early investors, especially the angel investors and possibly the founder, who may not have the resources to follow on. This is a very tricky situation for the founders as what could follow after the transaction is for the main investor to replace the founders and steer the company in a different direction, on a new vision that is no longer shared by the founders, who may lose control or possibly even the company that they founded.

Fundraising Paradigm #5: Don't Celebrate

So, we have just completed raising some money for our new venture. Do we pop the champagne? I often see startups raising their glasses and telling everyone that they have raised xxx dollars, as if raising money was the point of running the business in the first place, with each successful raise adding to the medal tally of the company.

I don't think that this is time to celebrate. Far from it.

In my previous ventures, my team and I did not allow the company to celebrate whenever we raised money. We did quite the opposite: we huddled everyone together and reminded ourselves that this was

---

45   Jon Medved, "6 tips to help you survive and prosper from the dreaded down round" OurCrowd (15 January 2023) <https://www.ourcrowd.com/startup-news/6-tips-to-help-you-survive-and-prosper-from-the-dreaded-down-round>.

money that didn't belong to us and that we were mere custodians of the funds that had bought us more time to grow. We were thankful for the trust from investors, for the hard work of the team. But we didn't celebrate as the company wasn't successful. Not just yet.

In fact, new challenges have just begun. Here are some of them.

Challenge 1: Founders Lose a Bit of Control with Each Fund Raise

With every injection of funds into a company, each shareholder's stake in the company is diluted to make room for the investor. The reduced share of the company by the founder can result in less control over the company and how it is run. It is also common for some investors to demand oversight of strategic decisions of the company and these are often captured in the section of the investment or shareholders agreement called "Reserved Matters".

Challenge 2: New and Additional Stakeholders to Manage

With new people on board, they would want to be updated regularly on progress or problems, and may be uninhibited in giving advice to the founders. This is a new normal for founders as they may be used to running the company by themselves, and being responsible for their own decisions. This new dynamic can initially feel stifling to the founders, who may need to adapt and build rapport and trust with the new investors.

Challenge 3: Beware of Personal Guarantees

If the investment is structured as a loan of sorts, the investor may require the founders to serve as personal guarantors to the loan. At the point of raising the funds, this might not seem like a big deal. After all, the founders expect the company to grow as they have predicted and everyone will be happy in the end. But this may not happen as predicted or hoped, and if things go south and the creditors come calling, the founders must be prepared to face the music. So, it is prudent that founders are fully aware of the consequences of acting as personal guarantors to any kind of loan to the company and they should decide if this is really what they are prepared for.

To Raise or Not to Raise, that is the Question

"他们不会雪中送炭; 他们只会雪上加霜" literally translates to: "They will not deliver coal in the winter, but will only add to the snow-covered roof". This was the experience that was related to me by an entrepreneur who had successfully raised some money from a VC. What this founder meant was that his investor didn't do much to help his enterprise other than with the money invested. Instead, the investor added more stress to an already stressful situation and he had to painstakingly manage this new normal accordingly.

I spoke with another co-founder and CEO of a major education chain that raised more than $20 million from a PE fund, to find out about her experience and position during that process. She told me that she had to hire top lawyers to help negotiate the deal and she was prepared to walk away if need be. "It was very expensive, but it got us what we wanted," she told me.

So, founders: talk to as many fellow entrepreneurs and other founders as you can to find out about the person you are raising money from. Don't jump at the first offer you get. And when you don't get any other offer, it may still be beneficial to hold out for a while more and pivot your business instead of getting help that may end up being a burden in the long run.

Being able to afford the expensive professional help and being able to walk away are attributes that only companies that do not need to raise money would have. This puts the company in a superior position to negotiate with investors who want in on the deal.

So, before we hit the market with a fundraising deck, wouldn't it be wise to evaluate if we are in that position to raise money first?

10

The Exit

Sell, Float or Close

In 1977, Roy Raymond and his wife, Gaye Raymond, opened a store in Stanford Shopping Center in Palo Alto, California, selling intimate wear (lingerie) for women. He wanted a store that offered a more upscale experience for shoppers compared to the typical department stores in the US. The concept caught on and the Raymonds opened a few more stores in the years that followed. In 1982, they sold the company and its six stores to Leslie Wexner, who owned Limited Brands, for $1 million.[46] Wexner revamped the company and took this concept to a whole new level, opening more stores worldwide and expanding the product line to include beauty products and clothing. By the early 1990s, the company had more than 350 stores throughout the US with sales of more than $1 billion. The company remained the largest lingerie retailer in the US as of 2021, with products sold in over 500 stores outside the US.[47]

The lingerie brand is Victoria's Secret.

46 Mary Hanbury & Áine Cain, "The rise, fall, and comeback of Victoria's Secret, America's biggest lingerie retailer" Insider (updated 6 March 2023) <https://www.businessinsider.com/victorias-secret-rise-and-fall-history-2019-5>.
47 P Smith, "Store count of Victoria's Secret in 2021, by region" Statista (3 November 2022) <https://www.statista.com/statistics/1341315/victoria-s-secret-stores-by-region/>.

Here's a thought: should Roy and Gaye Raymond have sold the company to Wexner so early on? If they had held on, even if the company was undergoing financial distress then, could they have reaped much more from Victoria's Secret than the $1 million they had sold it for to Wexner?

***

By now, you would be quite familiar with my second venture that started as a company no one knew about to one that led the market with a B2B service offering few thought was feasible, and it grew at a pace even fewer thought was possible. Our work made the news every two months. Our brand became synonymous with the industry in which we operated. Then investors came knocking on our door.

In the third year of the venture, I received an offer to acquire the company for a few million dollars. It was modest to say the least, especially for a company whose revenue grew by more than 20 times within two years of operation. Given the traction we had, surely we were worth more?

Should I have sold the company then?

***

You had a dream to change the world, so you started a venture to test your idea. Maybe your hypothesis was correct and you built good traction and charted an impressive revenue growth path, along with good profitability. Maybe your assumptions weren't correct and you couldn't find a product-market fit, so you went back to the drawing board and started over. It's been at least 36 months since you launched your venture. You are now at a crossroad where you can choose to exit the company or continue to raise more money to grow it, or to sustain it until you get a big break.

Should you exit the business now? How do you exit?

In this chapter, we explore three options available to founders when thinking about an exit: to list the business on a stock exchange, to close the business or to sell the business.

Option #1: Going Public

I won't discuss the merits of becoming a public company on stock exchanges like Nasdaq (USA) or the SGX Catalist (Singapore), which are more relevant to young and smaller companies. There are many well-documented success stories of founders who made it on Nasdaq with hundreds of millions of dollars in net worth. There are more advisors and an even greater amount of information on the internet that will give us a good sense of what the process is like.

I will discuss the aspects that few people talk about, like how the process of going public can impact the founder when things go south after listing and what to look out for in order to avoid getting stuck. Let's be clear, the founder will and is expected to get stuck with the company after it goes public, but we should try to avoid getting stuck to the extent that we end up benefiting everyone else on the Cap Table and be the last one to pick up the pieces when the show ends.

Going Public is Just the Beginning

Many things can happen to the stock price of a company in its first year of IPO, with the most drastic being stock prices that swing several folds in a matter of weeks. For example, one of the companies that were listed on Nasdaq in July 2022 saw its stock price shoot up by close to five times between 27 July and 2 August 2022, before tumbling more than 60 per cent by 10 August.[48] While such wild swings in stock prices are unusual for large cap stocks, the founder and entrepreneur who isn't familiar with the capital markets needs to be primed for such shocks from time to time for small cap stocks, especially during their first year of IPO. Since the founder will still be serving the moratorium during that time, they will need to carry the

---

48 · Bloomberg, AMTD:US <https://www.bloomberg.com/quote/AMTD:US>.

company through such fluctuations, manage sentiments and stabilise the ship. But if they can hold on and grow the company during this period, then going public may just be the beginning of a longer but possibly more exciting journey for the venture and its founder.

At the end of the day, if a company is built on firm fundamentals, has an ADO that is gaining traction, boasts great returns on investments, then the founder shouldn't be too concerned with these movements but should be focused on bringing the company to new heights going forward. And because the founder is able to sell his or her shares of the company after the moratorium period, they can choose to exit at different degrees by then.

Different exchanges have different rules to get listed on them. Assuming that a company qualifies for listing on a few stock exchanges, it will be worthwhile to think about the following:

- What is the liquidity in that market? Shareholders of companies listed on stock exchanges that are less liquid would find it harder to sell their shares as there are invariably less interest from fewer buyers;
- How relevant is your product for the market? Since it is likely that a substantial portion of the investors reside in the market where your company is listed, if the company's products are not relevant or if the company does not have a mechanism to make its products relevant or at least known to that market, it could be a challenge to attract investors there; and
- Is your company prepared for the potentially high listing cost and the much more stringent compliance requirements after it's been listed on a stock exchange? Maintaining a listed company is expensive and the company will need to set up a whole new team that is led by a qualified CFO. Thus, if the company's cash flow is unable to support the costs, it should consider other options to grow or exit the business.

There are many other considerations and getting a professional such as an investment banker to facilitate the process is essential. But the point is that an IPO by itself isn't an exit ticket *per se* but the start of a process to take the company to a different level, where its shares can be traded in public. And the founder will need to adjust his or her paradigm accordingly.

Option #2: Closing Shop

I started this book with a thought that some may disagree with: it is better to close shop and start over than to hang on to a company that is not making enough to fly and not losing enough to die.

Think about this: as an entrepreneur or a founder who wanted to solve a problem that you thought was huge, you invested all your resources, time and energy into building this business, only to find, three years after starting the venture, that the problem didn't seem as big as you had originally thought. Or perhaps your solution didn't seem awesome enough for people to want to buy it or enough for you to make good money. Or despite trying over and over during that period, you didn't seem to get it right.

Should you close shop and start over, or should you hang on?

This is a tough call and as an entrepreneur myself, I can say that it is like abandoning my own child whom I have nurtured with everything I've got. Give up? That's not in the vocabulary of a true entrepreneur.

But is closing shop giving up? Or is it a reset of vision, intent and paradigm for the founder?

You see, from my experience, staying in a business that is in "zombie mode" actually cements the founder to a "stuck" position, and the founder has no headspace of think of breakthroughs because he or she is preoccupied with how to make ends meet on a narrative that doesn't make the situation better the next month. This stifles innovation and destroys morale. It can even cause depression and if the founder feels alone in the fight and isn't well supported by the people around, it could spell a dangerous outcome for him or her.

Closing shop may actually present an avenue for the founder to reset and restart, and if this is done while the founder is still in good spirits, the entrepreneurial DNA in him or her will spur them to start again.

Sometimes, closing a business that is stuck in limbo is justified and I may argue that it is a wise decision if there isn't enough fit with the market, despite the best efforts from the founders and their teams. Deciding to close shop is not a sign of failure but one of maturity.

The comeback kid who showed the true spirit of enterprise – Nanz Chong Komo

Nanz Chong Komo founded the One.99shop in 1997 and grew it from a single store in Singapore selling low-priced items to a $14 million business with more than 20 stores. That was in 2000. Then SARS struck. Sales plunged. And in 2003, the company went into liquidation. She was declared bankrupt and only discharged in 2009.[49] But the entrepreneur in her didn't stop. She was determined to use her experience to inspire and help other entrepreneurs. So she wrote three books, started her own consultancy business and, in 2017, started Komo Pte Ltd as the exclusive country distributor of SodaStream in Singapore, a Pepsico brand.[50] Like many entrepreneurs, she started hustling and selling at an early age, helping in her parents' store while growing up in Hong Kong.[51] In an interview with the magazine *8Days* and in her books, Nanz shared openly about the lessons she had learned in the One99.shop venture that failed and how this has shaped the way she would do business in the next venture.

I wonder what would have become of her if she hadn't been able to close her business, allowed to reboot, reset and rethink her path as an entrepreneur, then to restart the journey, this time with the wisdom and the experience that can't be learned from a textbook, an online course or an MBA programme.

49   Nanz Chong Komo, "About Nanz" <https://nanzchong.com/pages/about>.
50   *The Straits Times*, "Turning Point: The rise and fall of entrepreneur Nanz Chong-Komo" <https://www.straitstimes.com/videos/turning-point-the-rise-and-fall-of-entrepreneur-nanz-chong-komo/5405944760001>.
51   Life Story, S1 Ep 7: "Nanz Chong Komo" (2006) <https://www.mewatch.sg/watch/Life-Story-E7-Nanz-Chong-Komo-64943>.

Option #3: Selling the Company
Why Sell?

Selling an enterprise we have founded allows us to cash in on our efforts expended over the years. Whether the efforts are successful or not depends on the lens through which we evaluate the business. For many of us, when we founded our first venture, we probably didn't have the money to set up our company properly and let it run smoothly. We needed to bootstrap and work insanely long hours for little to no wages, and had to convince others to join us in our crazy cause. With a nice exit and some money in hand, we can start our next venture and be its pre-seed investor to get it off to a better start than we did with our first venture.

I can think of five benefits for a founder to consider in relation to selling his or her venture as early as within 36 months of starting it, if a suitable buyer can be found:

1. <u>**Looking really good**</u> – If a founder can prove the capability of building a company and selling it within 36 months of inception, then it says a lot about his or her ability to go through the whole process of starting up, ramping up and exiting, all done at lightning speed. This is a very attractive attribute of a founder.
2. <u>**A lot easier to raise money in the next venture**</u> – With this kind of track record, investors are more likely to trust the founder's assessment of a new opportunity and believe what he or she says about the next venture idea, having "been there, done that" in the first venture.
3. <u>**Having money in hand**</u> – It gives the founder the power to put in the first set of seed capital needed to start the next venture on Day 1 without having to raise money from third parties. This gives investors the assurance that the founder has enough skin in the game. It also gives the founder some runway to build the venture to a level that shows convincing proof of concept with

the right metrics to stage a sizeable round of investment from savvy investors at the right time.

4. **Having the means to launch the next business idea quickly without investing time and money to build the offering** – With cash in hand, the founder can licence, acquire and invest in components or in other companies that make up the ecosystem needed to launch the new product in, say, two months or less, versus spending 18 months building something.

5. If the founder intends to stay on in the business to lead it to the next level and the buyer agrees, then selling it to a well-resourced buyer could remove the headache of having to ensure money is always available to sustain the business. This load off the shoulders of the founder can be a big incentive to sell the company and still retain some upside when the company gets to the next level.

When we sell our business, we typically get cash for the sale or receive shares from the buyer in lieu of cash. If we are offered shares in lieu of cash or a mix of both, then we should evaluate if the buyer has plans to make those shares tradable in a public market (going to IPO) or will be acquired by another company that intends to pay cash for the latter transaction. The whole point of thinking through these elements is to evaluate if we will ever get cash out of the transaction. If the answer is "yes", then perhaps it is worth a shot if the price is right. If the answer is "no" or "maybe", then we should think twice and assess if there are better alternatives.

What do Buyers Buy?

Buyers don't just acquire a business, they acquire the business's ability to do certain things (its core competencies), its product range, its customer base (the ecosystem), its brand or goodwill, its distribution and partnership network. Or buyers may simply acquire a business that is competing with them. The more the attributes of a target business contribute to the future revenue of a buyer, the more valuable it is to the buyer. So, buyers may want to look first at the revenue traction of the target company and how the revenue of the target can grow before they approach to make an offer. More importantly, how much more the revenue of this target business may grow if the buyer puts in its expertise, network, ecosystem and other assets to help it after the acquisition.

If the strategic assets of a company isn't revenue generating yet but are still attractive to the buyer, then the buyer may evaluate the merit of a potential acquisition along the lines of the following questions:

- Is it difficult to build the same assets independently, without spending money to acquire this business? Assets could mean protectable intellectual properties (IPs), brand value, network, goodwill, channels, etc.
- How long would it take to build those assets? Is it possible to wait that long?
- How much would it cost to build those assets? Would it cost more than the price to acquire the business? What is the price needed to be paid (the opportunity cost) to build those assets?
- Is the company in distress? Can it be bought at a really low price?

It is likely that a potential acquirer may start with an investment into the company as a corporate venture investor (see Chapter 9 "Raising Money for the First Time") and start some collaborations to test its capabilities, before making an offer to acquire a controlling stake.

The Selling Postures

Posturing and positioning correctly can make or break a potential sale. Here are some postures to consider when courting and negotiating with a prospective buyer.

Posture One: Don't show any signs of distress when dancing with a strategic buyer. I am quite certain most of us who are in business already know this, so I am aware that this is stating the obvious. But what I am really trying to say is: be open to and start thinking of selling the business as an option when you're doing well and not when the situation is dire. And if you need to sell your business when it isn't doing well, you will need to position it for a fire sale while aligning what you have to what the buyer really wants. This posture is important. Where possible, try not to let the buyer sense that you're more distressed to sell than to collaborate. The more the smell of distress emerges, the less leverage you will have as a seller. The more strategic your narrative is for a merger or a downright sale, the better starting position you will be in, which leads me to the next point.

Posture Two: Position the business to fit the potential buyer's narrative, by aligning the company's core capabilities with what the buyer needs. We can take a leaf from how Robert Iger of Disney managed to get Steve Jobs to the table to discuss strategic partnerships, leading to Disney acquiring Pixar (see Chapter 6 "Bootstrapping – Beg, Borrow, Build, Deal"). Whatever is the intent of the acquisition, whether to gain access to your customer base to get into a new market, or to own your tech to augment its current offering, you need to know how to align the core assets of your business to their goals. There is no straightforward way to know this and you cannot second guess your way to know the prospective buyer's interest, motivation or agenda. It comes down to the good old traditional way of getting to know the decision makers on the buyer's side, and observing what they have been doing to other companies they invest in to get a sense of their ambitions, dreams, vision and financial appetite. Then, armed with these insights, find the right time to propose a strategic acquisition of your enterprise. If they are amenable to this proposal, then the process of courtship begins, typically through a collaboration to test the fit.

This would give you some revenue while both parties can assess if they can work together to make something bigger.

Posture Three: Be a formidable threat to the buyer, even if you're not making money. When I say "threat", I don't mean a business that can outcompete the target buyer or even disrupt its business. To be threatening enough for a target buyer to take notice, your business only needs to be in a position to significantly affect one or two parts of the buyer's business. It could be that you have a significantly large user base whose users also happen to use the target buyer's products and it is plausible that you could offer similar products in due time and cause some form of migration from the target's customer base to you. Or you may have a piece of technology that could help the target buyer's competitors get ahead in the competition if they possess it.

Posture Four: Let the buyer know how much more there is to gain if it acquires your company and pumps in its current resources to grow it further. Some buyers, including some domain-specific PE funds, already possess strong domain or executional capabilities in their ecosystems that enable them to quickly scale a business that they acquire to a whole new level for an exit. In this situation, the prospective buyer may be looking for undervalued assets to acquire for a nominal price, then pumping in the resources to scale the acquired assets. In such situations, try to negotiate for a role in the leadership after the acquisition, provided you and the buyer are both aligned in vision and culture. Otherwise, if the price is right, you could consider taking the money and moving on to something more exciting.

Acquisition of WhatsApp by Facebook (now Meta) in 2014 – crazy move or the wisest one ever?

Meta (then Facebook) acquired WhatsApp for a whopping $19.4 billion. At that time, many thought this was a bold move with a sizable pinch of craziness. After all, WhatsApp's half yearly revenue was only slightly less than $16 million and it was still making incredible losses, although most of those losses were attributed to share-based compensation.[52] So, what was the rationale for this super high enterprise value in WhatsApp? Analysts who took a deep dive into the metrics of WhatsApp and the demographics of its users might have caught a glimpse of what had gone on in the mind of Mark Zuckerberg when his company made the acquisition offer, perceiving WhatsApp as both a threat and an asset for Facebook:

- **As a threat:** In April 2014, WhatsApp was already having 500 million monthly active users (or MAUs) and adding 1 million more daily. As of April 2022, WhatsApp was reported to have more than 2 billion MAUs. WhatsApp was also fast replacing the SMS as the means to communicate, and was a direct competitor to Facebook Messenger. Having a competitor to Facebook getting to WhatsApp first and owning those users may be unthinkable to Facebook.

- **As an asset:** WhatsApp's users are an asset for Facebook, which boasted 2.8 billion MAUs at the end of 2020.[53] The combined user base is a huge moat for a competitor to cross. What's more, WhatsApp is growing fastest in developing markets, with India, Brazil and Indonesia as the top three countries with the most users, accounting for close to 700 million users.[54] WhatsApp's design for the mobile device also primes it for further growth. These are valuable assets for Facebook.

While it remains to be seen if the acquisition of WhatsApp will justify the price, analysts seem to think that this could be one of the wisest, albeit the boldest, move in the tech world.[55]

52 US Securities and Exchange Commission, "Form 8-K/A, Facebook Inc" (date of report 4 October 2014), pp 53 & 59 <https://d1lge852tjjqow.cloudfront.net/CIK-0001326801/1f57fd25-66b8-42e6-89e9-c28725d215da.pdf>.

53 Meta Investor Relations, "Facebook Reports Fourth Quarter and Full Year 2020 Results" (27 January 2021) <https://investor.fb.com/investor-news/press-release-details/2021/Facebook-Reports-Fourth-Quarter-and-Full-Year-2020-Results/default.aspx>.

54 Daniel Ruby, "Whatsapp Statistics 2023 – How Many People Use Whatsapp" Demand Sage (2 February 2023) <https://www.demandsage.com/whatsapp-statistics/

55 Alison L Deutsch, "WhatsApp: The Best Meta Purchase Ever?" Investopedia (updated 29 March 2022) <https://www.investopedia.com/articles/investing/032515/whatsapp-best-facebook-purchase-ever.asp>.

To Sell or Not to Sell
The Offer that Got Away

Back to the acquisition offer for my venture in life sciences enrichment services that started this discussion. To qualify, that venture was a traditional service business, teaching children life sciences and biotechnology. And it was a cash business. It wasn't anything high tech or fanciful, nor did it look scalable. But we made it trendy at that time when we showed the world how children of all ages would learn complex concepts that most thought could only be learned at a much older age. We showed the education industry the possibilities and the potential of how much deeper understanding of complex concepts children could attain if we deployed the right method and resources. This was all very new and almost enchanting to educators, parents and the ministries of education we talked to. Plus, I owned 100 per cent of the company. No investors and no expectation or idea of what scaling actually meant (the term wasn't that common at that time). So a few million dollars was a lot and it was enough to have enabled me to buy a few apartment units in a very good residential district.

But I turned it down.

"A few millions to get the whole company for its innovative abilities and potential for growth is tantamount to an insult," I thought. I figured that I could grow my venture to $50m in revenue and we could be listed on the stock exchange. And we could make a lot more money with a nice exit that way.

So we decided to reinvest all of our profits into the company to create new offerings and open new markets because I could foresee that our then successful business model would run its course in time and we needed other revenue engines to buffer any decline in business. We also wanted to raise the barrier to entry in this space while we were still leading the pack.

But I had grotesquely underestimated the cost of all these new developments.

Fast forward to five years later, the company's revenue had plunged by more than 50 per cent as competitors quickly caught on and entered the market. To make things worse, our customers (education institutions then) decided to be our competitors. We started many regional joint ventures, raising money from investors, both institutional and individual angels, and in three years we had to close all of them because our original assumptions that things would work in those regional markets as they did in our home market were all wrong. Unlike the large singular markets of the US and China, our home market was very small to sustain any decent growth and the regional markets were too fragmented by culture, practices, lifestyle and policy to have the same strategy working there.

The Offer Rejected

In the summer of 1998, co-founders of Netflix, Reed Hastings and Marc Randolph, were invited by Joy Covey, Amazon's CFO, to Amazon's office to discuss partnership possibilities. Netflix had just started selling and renting DVDs and wasn't making money. Netflix needed to raise money to extend their runway. Amazon had raised $54 million from its IPO in 1997 and was on the lookout for good deals that it could acquire to grow its business. In a candid account from Marc Randolph's biography *That Will Never Work: The Birth of Netflix and the Amazing Life of an Idea*,[56] he described how the meeting with Jeff Bezos, the founder of Amazon, led to an informal verbal observation from Joy Covey that if Amazon did eventually acquire Netflix, it would be "somewhere in the low eight figures", which Randolph figured would be something between $14 million and $16 million. Not too bad for 12 months' work as CEO, according to Randolph.

The two founders of Netflix discussed the prospect of selling to Amazon at that price but decided not to sell in the end: Reed Hastings felt that Netflix could be worth a lot more than his previous venture

---

56   Marc Randolph, *That Will Never Work: The Birth of Netflix and the Amazing Life of an Idea* (Little, Brown and Company, 2019).

Pure Atria, whose IPO deal was already valued at $138 million. Randolph agreed with Hastings and no acquisition deal was struck with Amazon.

We know today that as of 2021, Netflix's market capitalisation was $250 billion and a formidable competitor to Amazon in the video streaming business.

Should the founders, Randolph and Hastings, have sold Netflix to Amazon at that time?

And would the Raymonds have been able to grow Victoria's Secret to become a billion-dollar company if they hadn't sold the business to Leslie Wexner's Limited Brands?

These are questions that I'm not even sure a gypsy with a crystal ball would have been able to answer at that time. If we follow the candid account of Netflix by its co-founder and first CEO, Marc Randolph, we know that prior to attaining such phenomenal success, the company had to go through a period where it needed to let go of staff, pivot, hang in there until it found the product-market fit, at a time when the stars aligned, to be where it is today.

It can be argued that Hastings already had one round of a successful exit at Pure Atria's IPO and thus would have had the experience, network and expertise to grow a company to a sizeable level for a decent exit down the road, and that the Amazon "soft" offer of the "low eight" digits would not be a fair value, given Netflix's potential under its founders, well, at least under the leadership of Hastings. In fact, Randolph, in his biography, mentioned that Hastings was already "a high eight-figure guy", fresh off Pure Atria's IPO.

Can we say the same of Roy and Gaye Raymond? I don't have the answer to this question, but it may be helpful to look at what we know of the Raymonds' track record in running Victoria's Secret. The Raymonds started the concept of high-end intimate wear for women, opened a store, did well enough to open a few more stores before the sale to Les Wexner, who took the company to a whole new level. Based on this observation, we can argue that the Raymonds might have lacked the necessary experience and international exposure in retail to have been able to bring the company to those new heights, which was something that Wexner, who was already building a retail empire when he bought Victoria's Secret,[57] was able to do.

Digging further into the track record of Roy Raymond, *The New York Times* reported in 1993 that Roy Raymond started a children's retail store called My Child's Destiny two years after the sale of Victoria's Secret. My Child's Destiny went bankrupt in 1986.[58] Maybe it was just bad luck, or maybe the Raymonds were wise to have sold Victoria's Secret in 1982 for $1 million.

The Deal We Got

Sometime in the early 2010s, my team and I conceptualised a way of presenting learning content in an interactive manner quite unlike anything the world had ever seen. Around the same time, Apple was launching the iBooks concept as an e-book killer. And the Apple iBooks samples were really quite a product to behold. Of course, iBooks didn't take off and Apple shut it down years later, which I have discussed in an earlier chapter. But the concept of an interactive book at that time was really novel and delightful to readers. The use case of our product was similar to iBooks. When we launched it in Singapore, we made news, which was good, for the reasons I have mentioned in Chapter 8 "Going to Market".

That was my fourth venture.

Soon, we got the attention of a large global education content company, whose CEO happened to be present at a seminar on the next generation of learning textbooks, where I was a speaker. He invited me to visit his office and meet his team, which I did three months later. After several discussions in the months that followed, both our companies reached a deal that included licensing the content

---

57 Mary Hanbury & Áine Cain, "The rise, fall, and comeback of Victoria's Secret, America's biggest lingerie retailer" Insider (updated 6 March 2023) <https://www.businessinsider.com/victorias-secret-rise-and-fall-history-2019-5>.

58 The Associated Press, "Roy Raymond, 47; Began Victoria's Secret" *The New York Times* (2 September 1993) <https://www.nytimes.com/1993/09/02/obituaries/roy-raymond-47-began-victoria-s-secret.html>.

from us for a fee and equity in a new spin-off to exploit the content, along with a generous contract for work by our team in Singapore.

Three years later, we exited that startup for a cash-for-equity deal. All-in-all, we made a decent few million dollars in this exit and had the resources to work on the next big thing for the company.

Here's the catch: this startup which we had exited from later merged with its major shareholder and the enlarged entity was listed on the stock exchange two years after we exited. The market capitalisation of the listed group was more than $100 million. At the time of listing, the startup contributed less than two per cent of the group's revenue.

Should I have held on and not sold our stake in the startup that early on? Would the value of our shares have appreciated significantly if we had held on? It's hard to say for sure.

In hindsight and having weighed all options available to us at that time, I like to think that the decision to exit was the right move. Here's why: we were struggling with adjusting to differences in work culture and expectations, and I had lost confidence in the team's ability to build a product that could scale nicely. Plus, we figured that the total amount of cash we would get from the exit and the goodwill that would be returned to us would have been worth the deal as it would provide us with the necessary monetary resources to work on the next big project.

By late 2010, the group announced that this startup's product would no longer be sold, effectively putting an end to the life of this startup, whose anchor product became subsumed into the group prior to its IPO, and eventually got buried. By then, we had already exited the startup for a few years.

Cash in Hand is Cash Indeed

I sometimes wonder what would have happened if I had sold the life sciences education business (my second venture) for those few million dollars shortly after we had gone to market. It was, after all, money in hand. And that is what counts, right? After all, I was then in my late 20s and just starting on my journey as an entrepreneur.

Perhaps my original hypothesis that the business venture could be worth $50 million or more in due course could have been true. But was I the leader who could have made this happen? It is quite likely that as an enterprise scale, a new set of leaders with different skillsets would be necessary to take it to the next level. Did I have the experience, expertise and persona to make that happen? From my track record of the five years following my rejection of that initial acquisition offer, it can be argued that I might not have possessed the necessary attributes to help my company scale to $50 million revenue at that time. But I guess no one really knows.

Of course, in hindsight, after that initial slump in business, I had pivoted the company to education technology and taken it to another level, raising funds and getting into all sorts of licensing deals that helped the company become very profitable in a new direction; there was even a nice exit in the early 2010s, as mentioned in the previous section. But then, I could have done all this as a new venture, with cash in hand from the earlier exit if I had accepted that first offer, right?

So, this is my take after all this:

Ultimately, the decision to sell should be guided by an honest assessment of the founder(s)' ability, network, experience and expertise to lead the company to the next level.

Otherwise, cash in hand is cash indeed.

Especially for first-time founders and entrepreneurs, I would recommend a paradigm that focuses on achieving a nice exit from a venture we have started, however small it may be.

And with the experience gained, and new money in hand, find another problem to start over.

Epilogue

The Tale of Two Edtechs

This book started with the story of two education technology companies, both hoping to raise funds for growth. Here are their profiles again:

AnalyzeEdu	LanguageStories
Four years old	Two years old
Offering tech to: • relieve teachers of admin work; and • check children's mental health.	Offering tech for online language learning in a fun and engaging way.
Word of mouth spread that led them to capture just ten per cent market share in four years, which suggests a low NPS or a lack of product-to-market fit.	NPS of 8.5 with low churn rate, suggesting that the offering is sticky and engaging enough for customers to promote to others. CAC: $250
Burn Multiple: < 1	Burn Multiple: 2
Annual Revenue: less than $200,000.	Annual Revenue: less than $200,000.
Planning to stay the course but open to ideas.	Fired most of the staff to stay afloat.

Based on what I have discussed in this book, I suggested to the founders of LanguageStories to double down and raise some capital to build on what they have achieved.

Here is my reasoning:

- A high NPS of 8.5 and a low churn rate is a great initial validation of product-market fit, suggesting that when the company's services are pitched to its customers, they love it.

		Low	High
Churn Rate	High	Serious problem with product-market-fit. Consider drastic redesign or pivot.	Product sales likely a one-time purchase model with few repeated purchases. Product is awesome enough for its owners to tell others about it.
	Low	Product is sticky, but not awesome enough to spread by word of mouth. Constant push needed to bring in new customers.	Product is sticky and awesome enough for users to promote to others. Product user growth at an inflection point, heading towards exponential growth.

Net Promoter Score

- The revenue is low and it suggests that the go-to-market strategy needs tweaking. It may be possible that the company has been spending too much money on things that don't bring in enough customers.
- The main challenge facing this company appears to be getting the word out there to the right targets on what the company has to offer. Possibly social e-commerce could work for them.
- As their service seems novel enough, the company should aim to present more innovative angles of their service or collaborate with a research body to study certain trends in language learning that

may benefit its model of teaching, and share such findings with the mass media to get the public's attention.

For AnalyzeEdu, I suggested a pivot, but pivot to what? Here are my thoughts:

- Despite being mildly profitable, AnalyzeEdu hasn't seemed to build traction on its product, gaining only ten per cent market share over four years with very modest revenue growth.
- Given that most of its customers learn about the company's product by word of mouth, and that the number of customers remains low after four years, it suggests that the NPS may be low and its customers are not loving it enough to recommend it to their friends. This, in turn, suggests a lack of product-to-market fit. I suggested that the founders do an NPS study to validate this hypothesis.
- A deeper dive into AnalyzeEdu's offering revealed that the offering might not be solving a big enough problem of its target customers – their teacher users did not appreciate the ability to do less administrative work as a powerful value proposition; it's not enough for them to tell their colleagues to adopt the product.
- AnalyzeEdu's core product does have one component that may be quite powerful, but for another industry – possibly the insurance market, where insurers hope to reduce the rate of mental stress of their young policyholders, and this solution could just help to monitor the state of their mental health.

"An Entrepreneur Never Stops"

This was what a founder of a successful business that was about to be listed on the local stock exchange told me when we were talking about the next big problem to tackle. Having been founders of our respective businesses, raised money from investors, grown our companies substantially and having managed staff from multiple locations across the globe, we both agreed that entrepreneurship was not for everyone. It takes a lot of guts, a solid vision and an unprecedented amount of grit mixed with a seemingly limitless level of optimism to start a new venture – to roll up our sleeves, get dirty in the mud and give it all that we have in the hope that our idea will change the world.

Yet, founders of new ventures in small fragmented markets like those in Asia, except for some large economies with spending power like China and Japan, may have it tougher than their peers in large, relatively homogeneous markets.

Small, Fragmented Markets Demand Quick Wins

The David versus Goliath narrative, where a small-time player is able to persist and win against a giant in the marketplace, is more likely to hold true in a market that is less fragmented and big enough to sustain many competitors, giving each its own space to grow over time. So, we see that many of the companies that have rejected acquisition offers in their early stages and eventually become highly successful seem to operate from huge markets like the US and China. These companies are not necessarily resident in these countries but they achieved success because they managed to break into these huge, relatively less fragmented markets.

A small market operates quite differently. Because of its low population and high business density (number of businesses over the population), the news of a company's success tends to spread quickly in this market. The company in a small market thus needs to run a lot faster to achieve a comparable level of traction that it would have achieved in a bigger market. And if there isn't enough runway for that company to build on its success, strengthen its moat and raise the barrier to entry into its space, then competitors can quickly enter the market and before we know it, we see our revenues plunging with a rapid loss of market share.

Because of this, a new venture founder in a small and fragmented market will need to ensure that the venture gains ground and market share quickly while the founder figures out different ways to exit in order to access a much bigger opportunity with the help of a strategic acquirer, or simply to cash out and find another problem to solve all over again in this small market.

Aim to Exit in 36 Months

This is also the main reason for me to recommend that a new venture should always aim to qualify for an exit event within a short period of time, such as 36 months after starting. This is especially so if the primary market is a small and fragmented one, like in Southeast Asia, the Middle East, Central Asia, Greater China or Africa.

This isn't everyone's cup of tea, obviously, and I have had friends telling me that 36 months is too short a period to build up something meaningful for a nice, big exit. Even if this may be so for some businesses, it is still not a good reason to avoid planning for it and pushing the envelope to aim for an exit in this short period of time. Just because many feel it cannot be done doesn't mean it is impossible.

In any business, there are the Reed Hastings (who led Netflix to become a multibillion-dollar enterprise) and there are the Raymonds (who probably felt compelled to sell Victoria's Secret). As founders, we need to be honest with ourselves and see if we have a Hastings team or a Raymonds team on board. And we need to be decisive about exiting our enterprise, whether by selling, floating or closing.

Because if our business becomes an "Outcome 3" business, one that makes too little to fly and too much to die, then it would be wiser to stop the pain, close it and return the money to our shareholders.

Then start over, now wiser, more confident and grounded.

So:

Startup with a goal to exit in 36 Months. Be the Fast Founder.

The entrepreneur who never stopped – A tribute to the Emporium Legend Lim Tow Yong (1925–2012)[59]

Lim Tow Yong, a Teochew native from China, came to Singapore in 1940 to join his brother in the provision and distribution business. Lim quickly became an eloquent and effective sales person and with Singapore emerging from World War II, there was a pent-up demand for basic necessities. The Lims' business in distributing such products from China, Germany and Hong Kong grew.

In 1961, the Lim brothers founded Emporium Holdings Group, based in Singapore to capture the rapidly growing retail opportunity here and in the region. Over the next 20 years, the Lim brothers opened 15 stores in Singapore and started expanding into many cities in Malaysia and Brunei. On one particular day, 28 March 1980, ten stores were opened simultaneously in Singapore alone. And by 1985, Emporium Holdings had 113 businesses spread all over Singapore, Malaysia, Brunei and Hong Kong.

However, when Singapore suffered the economic crisis in 1985, demand in stores plunged and by mid-1985, Emporium had suffered a loss of $10 million. With creditors and banks seeking repayment, Emporium was sold to Malaysian tycoon Bill Ch'ng two years later. One year after that, in 1989, Lim was declared bankrupt. He was 63 years old.

Many in his shoes might have given up altogether, thinking that they were already in their twilight years and might not have the energy to start over. Not Lim. The feisty entrepreneur never gave up on a comeback, and started another chain of departmental stores in Sabah, then in Brunei and Labuan. In 1999, Lim was discharged from bankruptcy. In the mid 2000s, Lim sold the department store chain and once again became a millionaire. He was 79 years old.

In 2006, Lim Tow Yong threw a dinner for all his ex-Emporium staff to thank them for standing by him through the years.[60]

---

59   Remember Singapore, "The Emporium Legend Lim Tow Yong (1925-2012)" (9 April 2012) <https://remembersingapore.org/2012/04/09/the-emporium-legend-lim-tow-yong/>.

60   The Star, "Ex-Emporium boss thanks staff who stood by him" (27 December 2006) <https://www.thestar.com.my/business/business-news/2006/12/27/exemporium-boss-thanks-staff-who-stood-by-him>.

Acknowledgements

The author would like to thank the following individuals for their influence on his journey as both an entrepreneur and an investor. Their examples as professionals and their partnerships with the author over the years have inspired many of the insights and stories shared in this book. The following names are mentioned in alphabetical order and not in any order of preference or importance.

Boh Wai Fong

An internationally-recognised expert in business innovation who recognised the innovativeness of my work, which has led to a great friendship that spans many collaborations to influence aspiring entrepreneurs to never stop innovating as they find new ways to solve old problems. Thank you for your friendship and the opportunity to work with you as a fellow thought leader in this exciting field!

Rodger Bybee

A world-renowned expert in Science Education who first recognised the value of my ideas and brought our work to the world's stage as a leading design in Science Education. It is an honour to count you as a dear friend and to have you as our advisor. Thank you for believing in my work and what it can do for millions of educators around the world!

Samer Elhajjar

An internationally-recognised domain expert in marketing who has been so kind to review my work and provide me with such valuable input on market sizing and definitions in this book. Thank you for elevating the quality of this piece of work!

Joan Hon

A noted science educator and multi-award winning novelist, who inspired me to think that I could change the world with text and the stories I tell and who always jumped to my help when I needed it most. Thank you for showing me how to write simply to express powerfully!

Low Khah Gek

Notably the most visionary education leader I know, whose eagle eye for opportunities to benefit her stakeholders made her one of the first collaborators in my earlier ventures, which led to an audaciously desirable offering that changed the world of learning forever. Thank you for your decisive leadership and the never-ending energy that continues to inspire me!

Tan Chin Hwee

One of the most visionary investors and successful professionals I know who was among the first to believe in my idea of a scalable venture. Every encounter with you has been a learning experience for me and so many parts of this book have been inspired by your sharing of experiences and your insights when looking at companies and leading one of the largest enterprises in the world!

John Teo

The kindest investor I know who never stopped believing that my work as an entrepreneur would benefit the world in ways I could not even begin to fathom, and who is the first to invest in my ventures.

Thank you for your advice, words of encouragement and always cheering me on!

Zhu Zhengdong

One of the most successful edtech professionals I know who taught me the wisdom of balanced entrepreneurship, and whose patience and belief in the work I do has helped one of my ventures scale to new heights. Thank you for showing me how to lead as an entrepreneur and for the great conversations we have!

About the Author

Eric Lam is a serial entrepreneur with Zero-to-One startup experience over the last 20 years, having founded and exited one of the region's most successful STEM edtech company and raised more than S$20 million from individual and institutional investors, including two public listed companies (listed on the NYSE and SGX Main Board). As CEO and founder, Eric inspired a team of more than ten nationalities across six offices worldwide to boost the startup's revenue by more than 20 times year-on-year, through some of the most innovative products in this part of the world. He also co-founded and exited an edtech startup in Australia within two years from startup to exit.

A venture innovator at heart, Eric has led teams within his current enterprise to set up new ventures in Asia Pacific and the USA, and has also invested and mentored startups in Singapore across various industries, bringing to the table substantial experience in achieving battle scars and triumphs in startup and scaling a business regionally, as well as in the USA and the Middle East.

His unique and poignant perspective on business design, opportunity identification, competition, entrepreneurship and learning has led him to be invited by MBA programmes and international conferences to share his narrative of rapid growth and disruptive competition against the big players in the market.